150 BEST TINY INTERIOR IDEAS

150 BEST TINY INTERIOR IDEAS

FRANCESC ZAMORA MOLA

HARPER
DESIGN
An Imprint of HarperCollins Publishers

HarperCollins books may be purchased for educational, business, or sales promotional use.
For information, please email the Special Markets Department at SPsales@harpercollins.com.

First published in 2021 by
Harper Design
An Imprint of *HarperCollins*Publishers
195 Broadway
New York, NY 10007
Tel.: (212) 207-7000
Fax: (855) 746-6023
harperdesign@harpercollins.com
www.hc.com

Distributed throughout the world by
*HarperCollins*Publishers
195 Broadway
New York, NY 10007

Editorial coordinator: Claudia Martínez Alonso
Art director: Mireia Casanovas Soley
Editor and texts: Francesc Zamora Mola
Layout: Cristina Simó Perales

ISBN 978-0-06-313891-9

Library of Congress Control Number: 2021020454

Printed in Korea
First printing, 2021

CONTENTS

INTRODUCTION

High housing costs, a fast-paced lifestyle, and increasing environmental awareness are quickly fostering a trend that changes the priorities that define the spaces we occupy. For some dwellers, it is no longer a goal to have a multiroom house with a garage and yard. The desire for extra space falls back in the list of priorities. Instead, dwellers find functionality and convenience more appealing.

One of the most noticeable movements that have derived from these habit changes is the rise of micro-housing. There is an urgent need for solutions that promote affordable housing in cities. Micro-housing is not simply about tiny living spaces. Living small for the sake of reducing our physical living environments isn't the point, and it is a gesture that would most likely be doomed to fail. Micro-housing, or reducing living environments to what some would consider tiny, is part of a larger system that favors increased social interaction; proximity to places such as work, school, shopping, and entertainment districts; and a sense of community and diversity.

But as some examples in the book show, the micro-housing trend is not unique to urban environments. Some are weekend retreats, off-grid cabins serving those in search of a little peace and quiet away from the noise of urban environments. This does not connote a living experience that is diminished or isolated. It is a lifestyle choice.

The demand for clever tiny spaces is motivating architects and designers to do more with less and capsize the misconception that tiny spaces are synonymous with cheap and lack of advantages. Reduce space doesn't mean reduce style. This book shows plenty of examples.

Most tiny living quarters include built-ins throughout—in the living area, the kitchen, the bathroom, and the bedroom. Built-ins make the most of limited space and offer flexible use of space, adapting the area to different situations. Built-ins also free space up, making it feel less cramped in favor of fluid circulation and seamless flow among contiguous areas. Open plans incorporating different functions are space efficient and allow for flexible use of the space available. Ample doorways or openings allowing sight lines through a sequence of spaces add a sense of amplitude and space unfolding. A palette of light colors and materials contributes to a warm and inviting ambiance while visually amplifying spaces, making them feel larger. Good lighting—both natural and artificial—and reflective surfaces also make tiny spaces feel larger than they are.

While moving toward smaller, space-efficient, and affordable spaces is an appealing move, providing homes that feel like they are one's private domain is critical. Tiny spaces don't necessarily sacrifice style. They can be functional, flexible, comfortable, and just as inviting—but in a more cozy way—as their larger counterparts.

Tiny spaces are a creative motivation for new construction, renovations, conversion of existing large spaces into smaller, more space-efficient ones, and technological advances in prefabrication. Building and planning regulations also adapt to contemporary housing needs, trying to mitigate the shortage of affordable housing. ADUs, or Accessory Dwelling Units, are on the rise, serving as guest apartment, home office, or additional bedroom.

These situations create a wide array of design opportunities, sometimes going beyond the typical residential typology. Yacht design and garage conversions into "in-law"/ ADU units are some examples. They demonstrate that some spatial expectations can be forgone in favor of practicality, convenience, and proximity to vital commodities.

Playfully dubbed "pied-à-mer," this apartment aboard a residential yacht by Michael K. Chen Architecture (MKCA) is simultaneously adaptable, efficient, and strikingly elegant. The residence serves as a holiday home for a couple and their grown children, transforming seamlessly from a spacious one-bedroom to a two-bedroom apartment through tables and beds that fold away and unfurl as necessary. Drawing from Le Corbusier's interest in streamlined, mid-twentieth-century steamship design, the space is also reflective of MKCA's own expertise in creating compact, multifunctional spaces in contemporary urban environments.

Pied-à-Mer

600 sq ft
Aboard a residential yacht

Michael K Chen Architecture // MKCA

© Alan Tansy

As a jumping-off point for the project, MKCA looked to modernist architecture's fascination with nautical design, which optimized for small-scale living, modular organization, and efficiency. In particular, Le Corbusier's belief that a home should be regarded as a "machine for living," as well as his fascination with cruise ships as models for self-sufficient, utopian apartment complexes, like his famed 1952 Unité d'Habitation, offered inspiration.

MKCA has included two bedrooms, two baths, a kitchen, a dressing room, a sitting area, a trunk room, and a landing zone. When needed, the dining area converts easily into the second bedroom, with the dining table tucking into the wall to make way for a sleek cantilevered fold-up bed. When converted into a two-bedroom space, a sliding screen divides the apartment, allowing privacy for guests. Two pod-like volumes, each containing private bath and storage areas, organize the apartment while retaining effortless movement through its common areas and from its front door to its broad, ocean-facing glass wall.

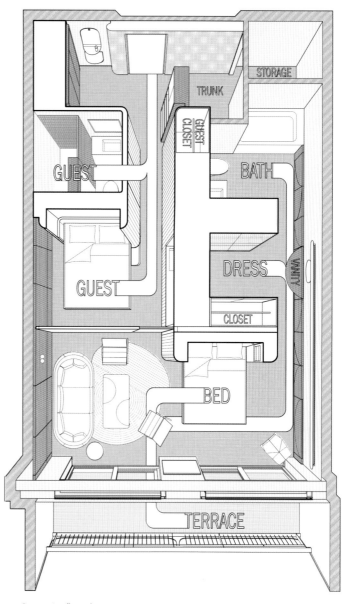

Perspective floor plan

Contemporary pieces were mixed with several vintage items, in largely natural materials and rich, warm colors, as a counterpoint to the cool blue and gray, slightly machine aesthetic of the custom-fabricated elements.

The ship's furnishings were specified in the spirit of collaboration, whether sourced from independent designers, commissioned or customized specifically for the project, or custom-designed by MKCA. Motion and a sense of spaciousness, are further encouraged through light and reflection.

001

Multifunctional furniture can adapt to different living situations, allowing for the transformation of spaces. The furniture is not only technically sophisticated but also very stylish.

Continuous aluminum ribs help conceal panel divisions, doors, and appliances, and also accentuate a sensation of height in the relatively low, 8-foot-tall space. Finishes throughout the apartment are either impervious or designed to patina over time.

002

Rather than flooding surfaces with spotlights, try backlighting solutions to light up shelves, mirrors, artwork, and ceilings, for instance. Backlighting can add modern appeal to any space, from entry areas to bathrooms.

Concepts of motion and multifunctionalism
underpin all aspects of the residence's
organization and aesthetic. In addition
to disappearing tables and beds, MKCA
has incorporated hidden lighting and
integrated appliances that can be boldly
revealed or neatly tucked away.

003

Pattern scale and color choices influence the way we perceive spaces. Small tiles and bright colors do make small spaces look larger. Also, small tiles are often preferred in bathrooms because there is less tile cutting involved around toilet seats, for instance.

004

Expand your horizons and be open to creative design ideas that can give the feeling of living large and in style in a small space.

Granny Pad

571 sq ft

Seattle, Washington,
United States

Best Practice Architecture

© Sozinho Imagery

The project began when the client couldn't find appropriate housing for "Granny" in their neighborhood. With a growing family, they didn't have enough space in their house to accommodate her needs and maintain the privacy everyone in the family wanted. And with a shortage of affordable housing in Seattle, the option of moving to a larger house in the city was out of reach. Best Practice saw converting the client's existing garage (previously used as storage) as the perfect solution. Design considerations included looking at the project on both a short-term and long-term timeline. First, Best Practice needed to address the immediate needs of the client. They also considered future uses of the space as a possible rental unit, studio, office, or other income-generating project for the family.

005

A limited selection of materials and colors makes buildings look more homogenous and less disarticulated. Buildings are therefore perceived as one entity rather than a composition of various parts.

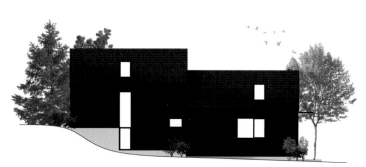

East elevation

North elevation

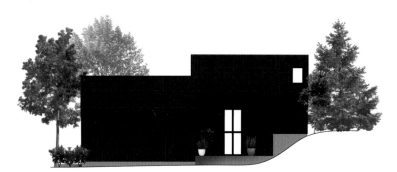

West elevation

South elevation

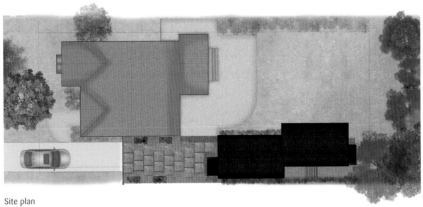

Site plan

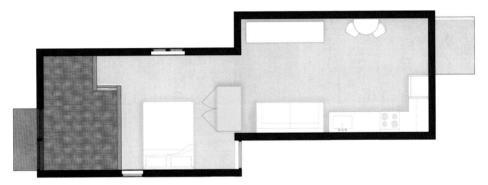

Loft level plan

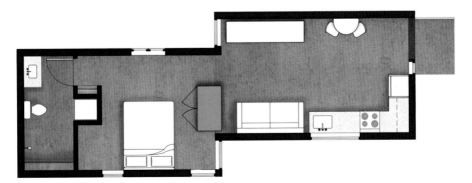

Main level plan

Section perspective

To accommodate the decreased mobility
associated with aging, the living area
needed to be one level. Rather than
make several small rooms, the team
opted to create open, central spaces
that can be easily adapted to changing
mobility issues.

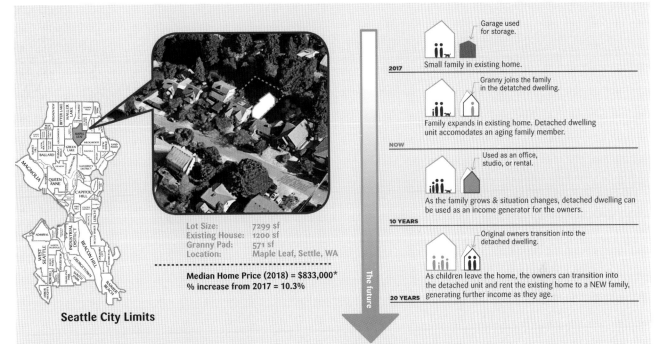

Seattle City Limits

Lot Size: 7299 sf
Existing House: 1200 sf
Granny Pad: 571 sf
Location: Maple Leaf, Settle, WA

Median Home Price (2018) = $833,000*
% increase from 2017 = 10.3%

The future

2017 Small family in existing home.

Garage used for storage.

Granny joins the family in the detatched dwelling.

NOW Family expands in existing home. Detached dwelling unit accomodates an aging family member.

Used as an office, studio, or rental.

10 YEARS As the family grows & situation changes, detached dwelling can be used as an income generator for the owners.

Original owners transition into the detached dwelling.

20 YEARS As children leave the home, the owners can transition into the detached unit and rent the existing home to a NEW family, generating further income as they age.

Granny Pad

* Rosenberg, Mike. *The Seattle Times*, "New Home-Price Highs..." March 6, 2018

ADU adaptability diagram

006

Large openings bringing abundant natural light into an interior space and allowing visual connection with the exterior expand the visual field.

007

The design goal was to maximize usable space without creating a cramped feeling: the existing garage door was removed, and the old structure became the entry, kitchen, and sitting room. A short walk through the entryway reveals the bedroom, closet with laundry, and bathroom.

008

Carefully placed windows and skylights provide lots of daylight. Rafters were left exposed in the ceiling. A lofted space above the bathroom—accessed by a ladder—will be used as storage for the time being but can easily be transformed into an office or sleeping loft in the future.

All of these details come together to create a soaring, open feeling that makes the relatively small footprint of Granny Pad feel much larger. Behind the structure sits a private back deck that connects to the loft space.

009

The view of an open plan from an elevated spot like a mezzanine creates the feeling of amplitude.

A young family of four wanted to update an original 1950s California Ranch home nestled above The Mesa. With a modest budget and an owner savvy in both construction and design, Anacapa Architecture was able to renovate the existing house and add 600 square feet of usable living space, including a new two-car garage and full master suite with a glass wall on the yard side. The interior of the existing house was opened up to allow a free-flowing space through the main kitchen, living, and dining areas, anchoring the open plan around a fireplace. Leading out to the owner-designed rear yard is a large sliding-glass wall that defines the indoor/outdoor connection California is known for. White finishes and cool woods lend a Scandinavian appeal to this classy and minimal space.

Vista de la Cumbre

Residence: 1,502 sq ft

Garage: 434 sq ft

Santa Barbara, California, United States

Anacapa Architecture

© Erin Feinblatt

Interiors walls were removed to create an open space with direct access to the outdoor patio.

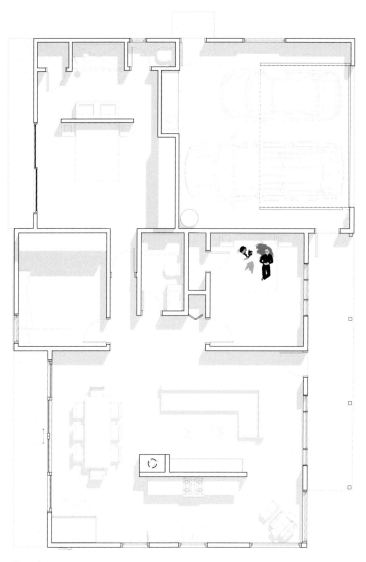

Floor plan

010

A central feature such as a fireplace can anchor different areas around it, avoiding the need for partitions to separate different areas.

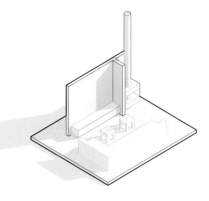

Living room axonometric view

011

Kitchens opened to living areas enhance the spatial experience—something that separate rooms can't do.

The remodel combines Scandinavian style with California style. One of the most prominent features are the steel windows, which add character to the minimalist home.

012

Doorways in place of doors wherever privacy isn't an issue will create a sense of spatial continuity.

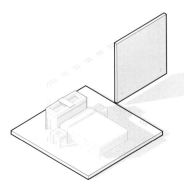

Master bedroom axonometric view

The courtyard is an outdoor extension of the living area, a place to relax or entertain surrounded by nature

In his Kammerspiel—intimate theater—the architect has playfully addressed the subject of "living in a small space" with one single large piece of furniture as a centerpiece. This piece of furniture, shaped like a cube, concentrates various household functions to maximize the openness of the space around it. Most domestic functions find their own specific place in the cube. Sleeping, eating, working, and reading are organized on the exterior sides, while everyday essentials, as well as a walk-in wardrobe, have their place in the interior. The composition of the cube can, however, be customized, adapting to the lifestyle and habits of the user.

Moormann's Kammerspiel

441 sq ft
Prototype

Nils Holger Moormann and B&O Group

© Julia Rotter

Design development sketches

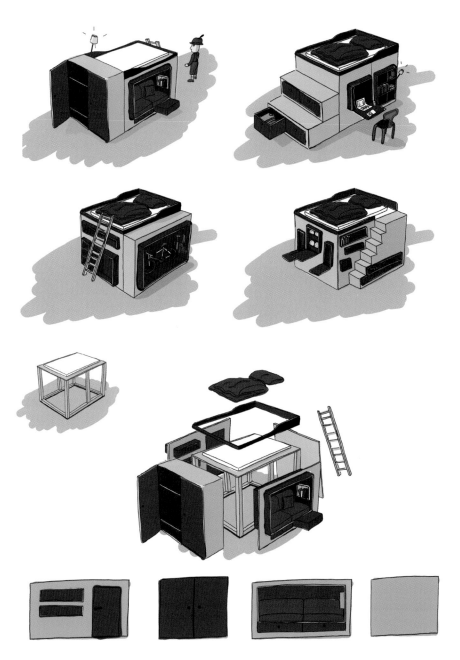

013

The cubic object set at a skew angle in the center differentiates functional use areas—the entry, the kitchen, the lounging area, and the dining/office zone. Each side then addresses that function. There is a place to hang the bike at the entry, a couch in the sitting area, and so on.

Design development sketches

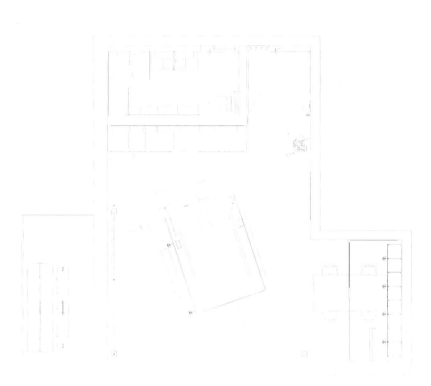

Floor plan

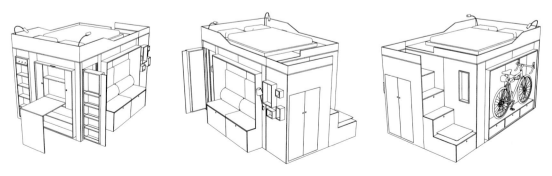

Axonometric views

014

The "Swiss Army knife" cube also provides a platform for hidden, indirect lighting. For general lighting, indirect is best, and it can be fairly inexpensive to use modern LED trims to accomplish this.

015

In any tiny space, the first necessity is organization. "A place for everything and everything in its place." This tiny space is exacting in meeting that requirement, leaving as much as possible of the most valuable commodity in small spaces: uncluttered open space.

The interior offers storage space for three drink crates, twenty-five wine bottles, a vacuum cleaner, and a cleaning bucket. There is also room for three compartments to keep cleaning supplies, a wall bracket for a snowboard or skis with a shelf for shoes and helmet, rails for six plastic boxes, and a clothes rack.

016

A limited palette of materials keeps small spaces from becoming too visually busy. Here, uncommonly, the ceiling and walls share the same finish. The floor is seamless and neutral—keeping with the theme of simplicity. Flat black millwork completes a triad of materials that run throughout.

Ashen Cabin is 3D printed from concrete and clothed in a robotically fabricated envelope made of irregular ash wood logs. The cabin lifts off the ground on 3D-printed legs that adjust to the sloped terrain. All concrete components were fabricated on a self-built 3D printer. The cabin utilizes wood infested by the emerald ash borer for its envelope, which is widely considered as "waste." By implementing 3D scanning and robotic fabrication technology, HANNAH upcycles infested "waste wood" into an abundantly available and sustainable building material. Architecturally, Ashen Cabin walks the line between familiar and unfamiliar; between technologically advanced and formally elemental. The undulating wooden surfaces are strategically deployed to highlight moments of architectural importance.

Ashen Cabin

100 sq ft

Ithaca, New York,
United States

HANNAH

© Hannah and Andy Chen

017

3D printing is slowly becoming an integral part of architecture, facilitating new construction forms and allowing for interesting architectural languages.

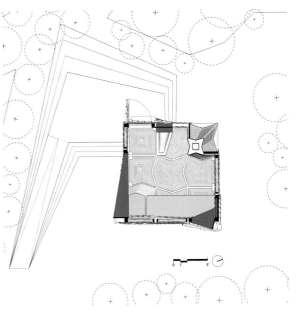

Site plan

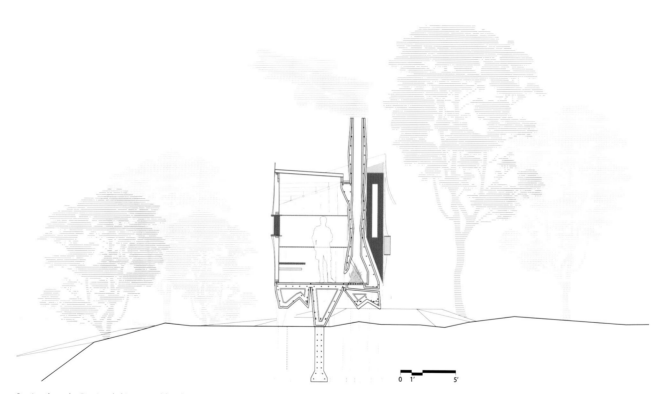

Section through 3D-printed chimney and fireplace

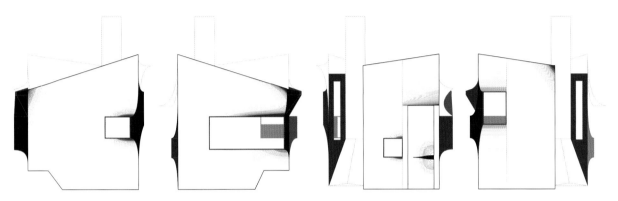

Unrolled elevation diagram

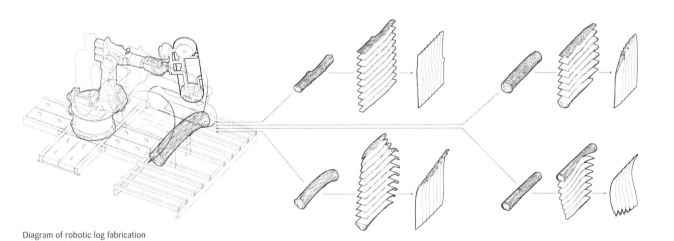

Diagram of robotic log fabrication

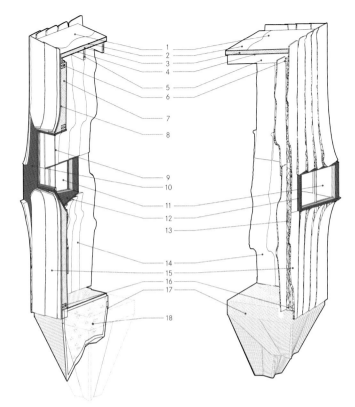

Detail axonometric of corner module

1. EPDM roof membrane
2. Roof coverboard
3. Rigid insulation
4. Plywood sheathing
5. 2x6 wood rafter
6. 2x4 integral wood top plate
7. Closed-cell spray foam insulation
8. Integral corrugated drainage plane
9. Fixed glazing
10. Plywood spandrel
11. Operable glazing
12. Plywood window box
13. Integral log post
14. Interior log sheathing
15. Exterior log sheathing
16. 2x4 integral wood bottom plate
17. 3d-printed concrete formwork
18. Poured concrete infill

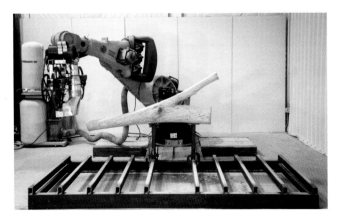

3D scanning and robotic fabrication technology were used to create with high accuracy the complex sculptural forms of the cabin.

018

The exterior cladding is carried out to the cabin's interior, creating a rough yet agreeable envelope. This interior is devoid of any ornament so as not to overwhelm the tiny interior and prioritize the textural quality of the space.

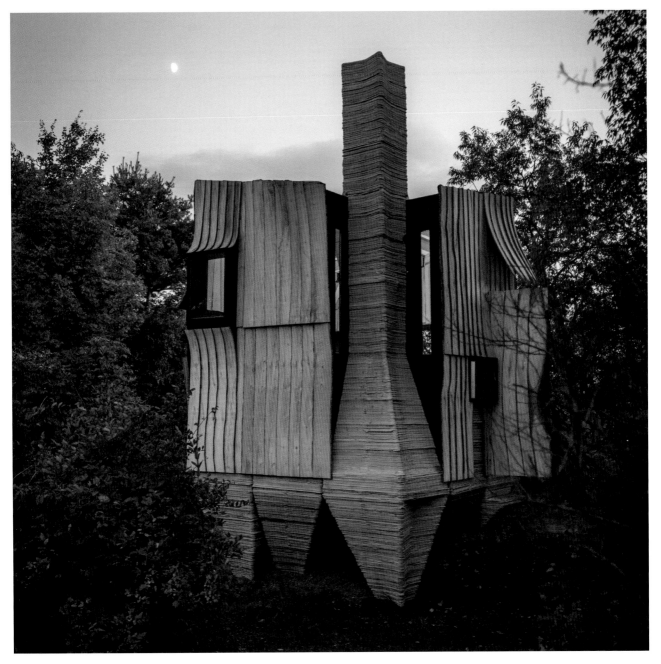

Long Estate

323 sq ft

Poznań, Poland

Mili Młodzi Ludzie

© PION - piondaily.tumblr.com

For the remodel of a townhouse's attic, the owners requested a living room with a kitchenette and a sleeping area with a bathroom. The usable space is optimized despite the long and narrow proportions of the space and the walls, and ceiling's irregular shapes. Because of the space constraints, the different areas had to remain in their original location, especially the kitchen and the bathroom. The remodel successfully satisfies the owners' requirements, upgrading the old attic to contemporary living standards. Enhancing original features such as the roof structure is evocative of the attic's original character.

019

The black wall, called "the ribbon," integrates a bathroom that separates the area dedicated to daily activities from the bedroom.

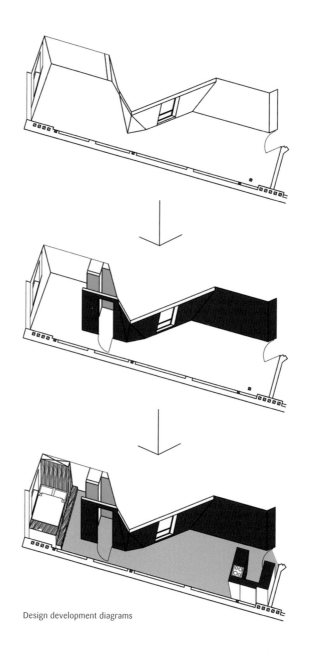

Design development diagrams

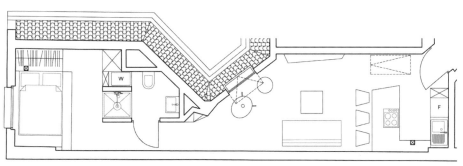

Floor plan

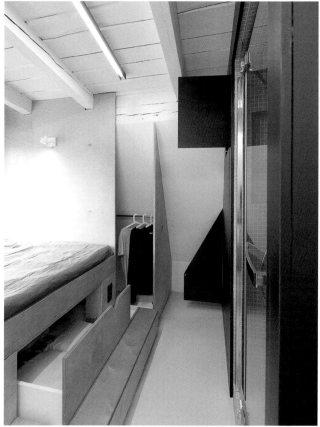

020

The raised bed platform is complete with various integrated drawers that add easy-to-reach linen storage.

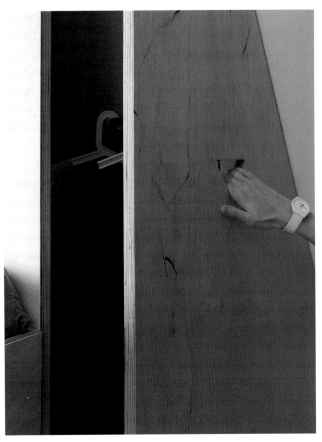

The geometry of the overall layout served as inspiration for the design of the kitchenette, the TV unit, and other integrated cabinets.

021

The shower, accessible from both
the bedroom and the bathroom,
has two glass shower enclosures
that let the light from the bedroom
window into the bathroom while
creating additional circulation and
adding practicality.

Peter's Apartment

280 sq ft

Poznań, Poland

Mili Młodzi Ludzie

© Lusia Kosik

The surfaces in Peter's Apartment are entirely white, from the resin flooring and paneling of the walls and ceiling to the minimalistic design of the kitchen. This immaculate decor is, however, disrupted by a series of grooves that trace the configuration of the cabinets. The lack of ornament enhances the minimalistic decor. A TV set, storage, a desk, and a kitchen are concealed behind the cabinet and panel fronts. Taking advantage of the high ceiling, a sleeping loft, accessible through a ladder, is stacked on top of the bathroom.

The lines crisscrossing the walls and ceiling of the apartment are generated by four imaginary intersecting planes.

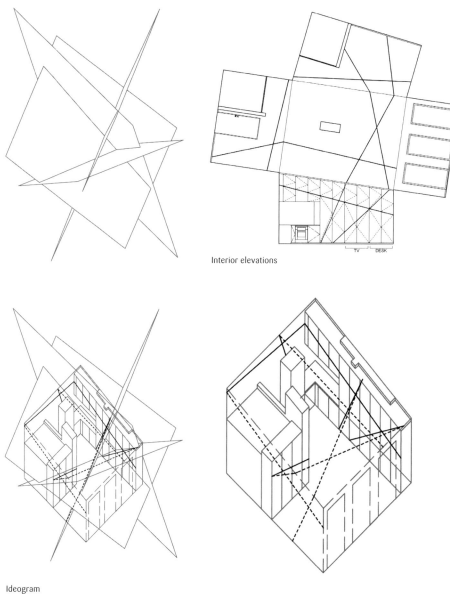

Interior elevations

Ideogram

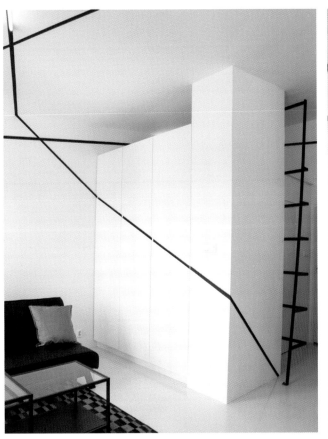

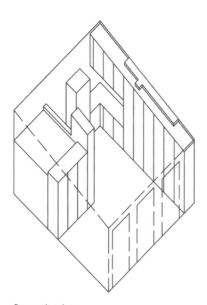

Perspective view

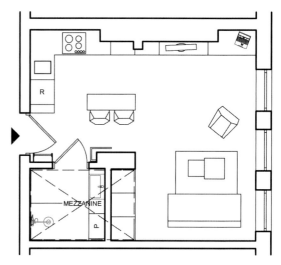

MEZZANINE

Floor plan

The minimalistic design includes materials such as resin flooring, white and black melamine fittings, powder-coated steel, pinewood, and ceramic tiles.

022

The loft bed above the bathroom is accessible by means of a black steel ladder. Its design echoes the dark shadow lines that crisscross the surfaces of the apartment. In terms of functionality, the loft bed is undoubtedly an effective space-saving solution for small homes.

Some cabinets are full height, while others are short of the ceiling, expanding the perception of the space, already enhanced by the cuts in the walls and ceiling.

Sparrow House

850 sq ft

Culver City, California,
United States

Samantha Mink

© Samantha Mink, Chad Slattery

The name of the house was inspired by a Chinese proverb: "Small as it is, the sparrow has all the essential organs."

The unusual and modest lot size and configuration on the one hand, and financial budgets on the other, set the initial limitations for the scope of the project. Due to planning restrictions, the footprint and square footage of the house had to remain the same. Located on a unique street, the house came with all the great potential of "a box," mundane and ready for a transformation. The result is a sometimes stern but multifaceted exterior, with an almost unexpectedly warm, bright, and comfortable interior. The house is small and simple, without room for stylistic and haughty gestures, but with just enough room for living.

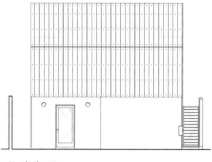

North elevation

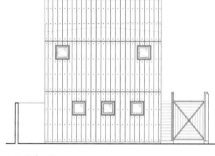

East elevation

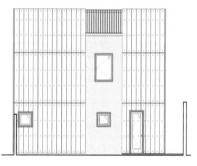

South elevation

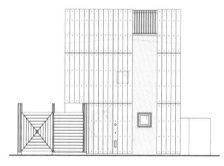

West elevation

Section

The fenestration was recomposed to control and direct the admittance of light by standardizing and shrinking all windows. The roof was sliced down the middle for new skylights and a hatch, which leads to the new landscaped and furnished roof deck. These simple moves create a clear contrast between the more articulated moments of light and the broad, sweeping light pouring in from above.

The exterior is clad with dark, wood boards—also standard lumber—whose black and brown textural depth transmutes throughout the day and in different light conditions. The exterior lattice, with newly planted bougainvillea, recaptures the original character of the house, which was covered in vines upon purchase.

While the footprint remained the same, all doors were reconfigured, including moving the main entry door off the street, facilitating a more indirect approach through a new garden.

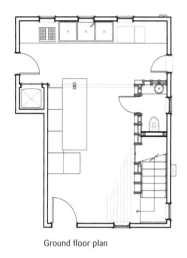

Ground floor plan

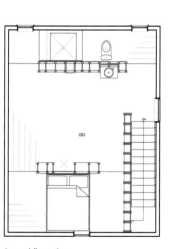

Roof deck floor plan

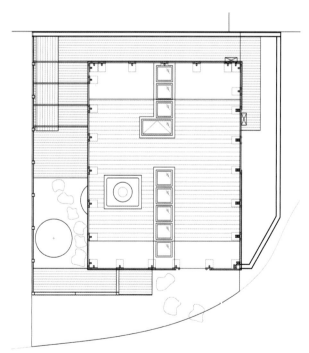

Site plan

Second floor plan

023

Customized millwork can make the most of every inch available while giving a home a unique character.

All interior walls were removed to open the space up, allowing for new exposed wood beams and columns, and new "thickened partitions" of functional wood cabinetry. All wood in the house is Douglas fir or pine, keeping costs low while bringing warmth to the spaces with its color and texture.

024

Roof decks are outdoor expansions
of living spaces.

Inhabited Wooden Walls

603 sq ft

Geneva, Switzerland

Aurélie Monet Kasisi

© Yann Laubscher

The owners of a family house wanted to create storage in two large rooms and divide each into two smaller ones to accommodate different household programs. Two "wooden walls"—one for each room—provide abundant storage and partition off the rooms to create a home cinema and a playroom in one room, a small office and a bedroom for an au pair in the other. The "wooden walls" are made of oiled pine. They sit on colorful feet made of recycled bricks and landscape edging pieces.

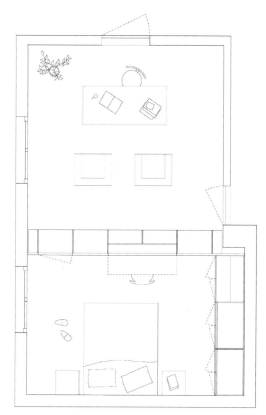

Office and au pair bedroom floor plan

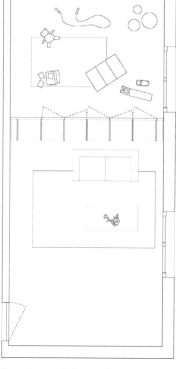

Home cinema and playroom floor plan

One of the bookshelves stores the family's CD collection and a beamer for the home cinema. Behind the bookshelf is the kids' playroom with a circular opening that adds a playful touch to the structure while allowing parents to keep an eye on their kids.

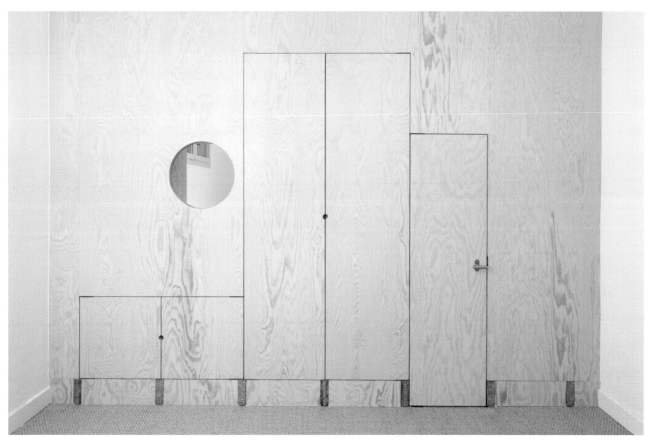

025

A series of small accessories,
including a movable wooden
stepped block in the playroom,
storage boxes, and nightstands,
were also designed to complete
the furnishing of the new rooms.

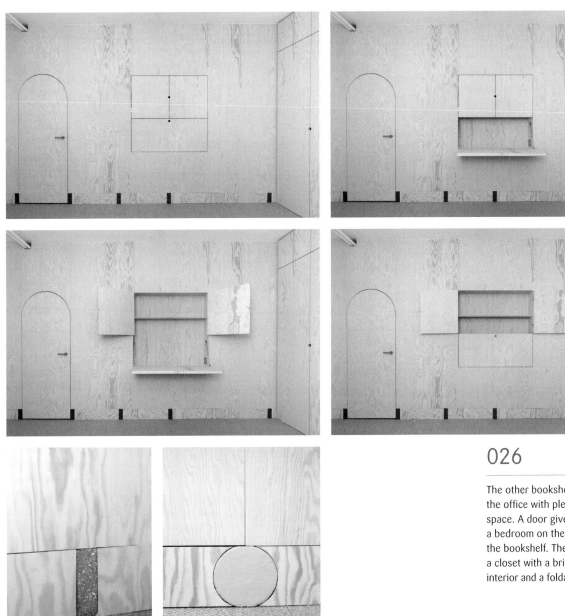

026

The other bookshelf provides the office with plenty of shelving space. A door gives access to a bedroom on the other side of the bookshelf. The bedroom has a closet with a brightly painted interior and a foldaway desk.

Our client, a ceramicist and artist, lives in a loft residence in a renovated manufacturing building in Providence. Although it is large, open, airy, and home to her studio, the loft lacks the outdoor space she desires for a balanced life. The request was simple: a cottage in the woods for our client to retreat from urban loft living, reconnect with nature, and develop a garden landscape with walking trails. The design challenge of this project is tight. The exterior of the cottage, a cubic volume measuring 25' × 25' × 25', is faceted like a gem. Facets are cut to shed water, carved into a protected entry, or shaped for a venting chimney. Like the rocks of the site, the cottage is an understated angular block that opens up in celebration of nature. The cottage's exterior is entirely clad in Alaska yellow cedar—a durable wood that has been left untreated and will weather to a silver gray.

Cottage in Woods

530 sq ft

Foster, Rhode Island,
United States

3SIXo Architecture

© 3SIXo Architecture

027

Small spaces can be full of
architectural character in their
massing and materiality.

Study models

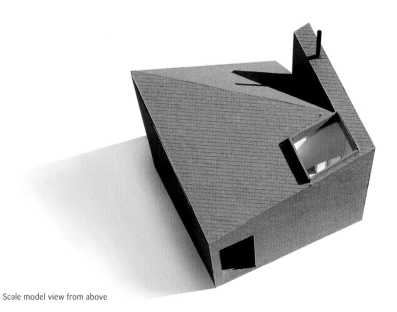

Scale model view from above

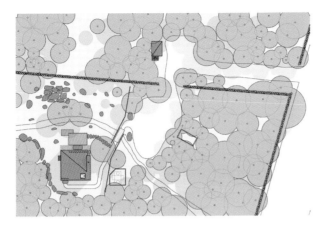

Site plan

From the large sliding doors, a stepping-stone sequence of Alaska yellow cedar decks and placed boulders create a series of outdoor living spaces that extend the cottage outward. The garden and terrace areas, created by arranging large boulders that were unearthed by the excavation, are bounded on the south by an existing fieldstone wall and overlook a small meadow.

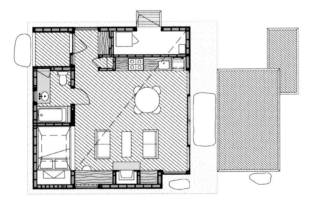

Floor plan

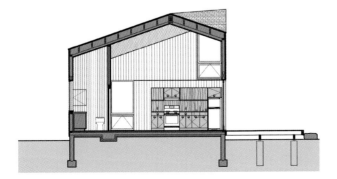

Section

The high corner window faces east for morning light. Aligned windows at the desk and entry allow views right through the cottage. Walls and ceilings are painted vertical pine boards laid with a small gap for the seasonal expansion of the wood, and floors are made of clear Douglas fir.

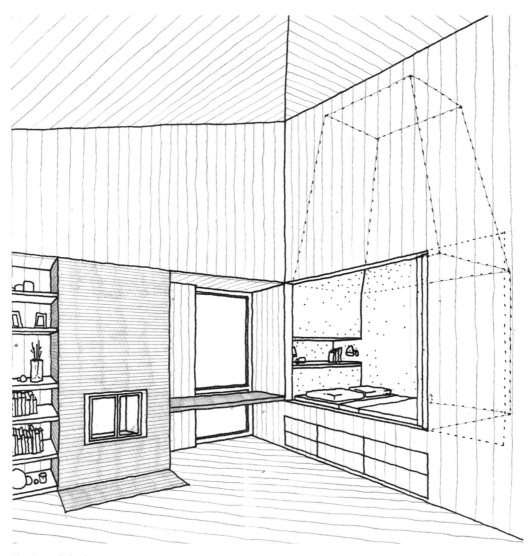

Sleeping nook sketch

The interior is one large cavity with its ceiling rising to the diagonal ridge at a height of 17 feet. The wide sliding-glass opening faces south toward the garden landscape and deck. A pyramidal shaft connects the sleeping nook to a skylight 14 feet above, making it an observatory at night and a light-filled chamber during the day.

028

Alcoves of Douglas fir carved
for the entry with a bench and a
desk with bookshelves maximize
functionality.

The entry door is painted bright red, a splash of color in the otherwise soothing coloring of the interiors. Cabinets and window frames are painted with gray enamel paint to contrast with the warm coloring of the Douglas fir.

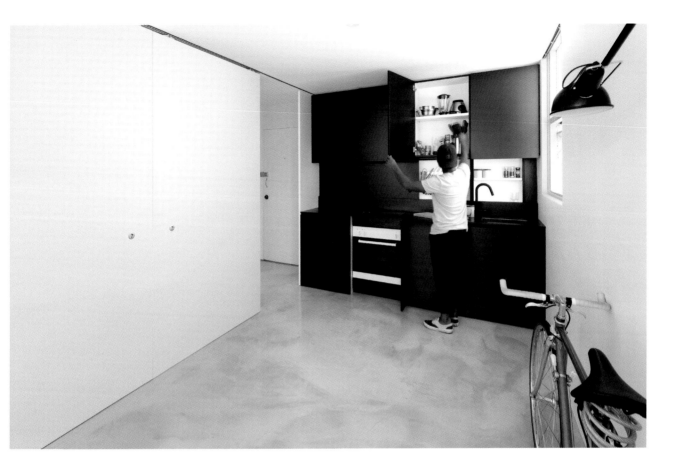

A wooden "pod" was inserted into an open space to address the issues of privacy, storage, and a lack of living space inherent to tiny apartments. The sturdy structure features full-height, wall-to-wall sliding doors, and accommodates an entry foyer, storage, washing, and sleeping zones. The studio's open quality provides an adequate setup for flexible use, while ingenious storage solutions keep the home tidy and organized.

The Studio

291 sq ft

Sydney, New South Wales, Australia

Nicholas Gurney

© Katherine Lu

029

The cabinet fronts, painted white
to blend with the walls and ceiling,
are conceived as skin that peels off
to reveal colorful interiors.

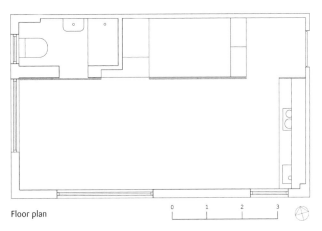

Floor plan

0　1　2　3

030

The black kitchen block contrasts sharply with the white surfaces. The lack of cabinet hardware highlights the design aesthetic based on colors associated with a specific function.

031

Space limitations discouraged the use of conventional kitchen drawers. Inner workings are completely out of sight, offering a clean look in line with the unadorned decor.

Architect's Studio

377 sq ft
Moscow, Russia

Ruetemple

© Ruetemple

A stimulating environment is capable of promoting creativity. This is what the owner of this former garage might have thought when he gave it to his daughter, an architecture student. A unique single piece of furniture is the focus of the transformation of the garage into a workspace and lounge area. The design was conceived to promote creativity. The open bookshelves are also partitions that reveal views of adjacent areas, like superimposed layers, offering an element of surprise that enhances the spatial experience.

During demolition, the dropped ceiling was removed to unexpectedly reveal a system of roof trusses worth incorporating into the design of the new workshop.

032

The dividers serve two purposes: provide plenty of shelving space and generate various areas of different functions in the way screens do. While the dividers break up the space into smaller areas, they do not interfere with the open feel of the gutted garage.

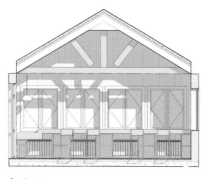

Section 1

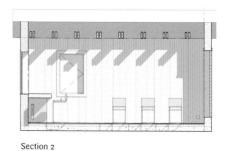

Section 2

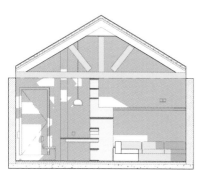

Section 3

Section 4

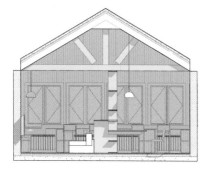

Section 5

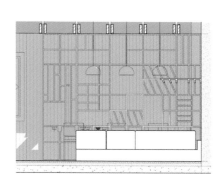

Section 6

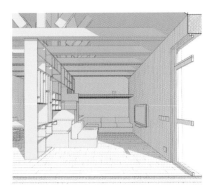

Perspective view 1

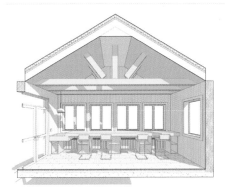

Perspective view 2

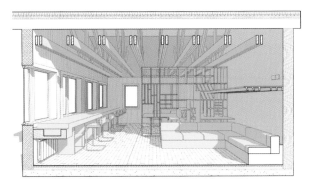

Perspective view 3

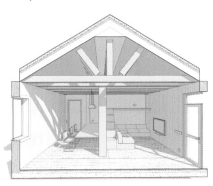

Perspective view 4

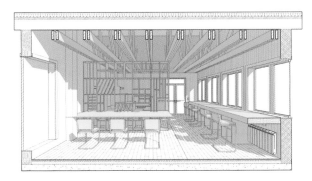

Perspective view 5

Axonometric view

033

A single piece of furniture generates various areas for different functions, integrating plenty of shelving, a desk, a sofa, and even a loft bed.

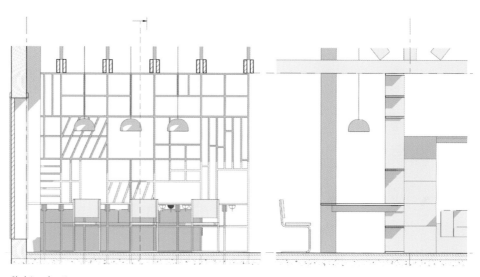

Shelving elevation

034

The piece of furniture is an open shelving system for easy access from two sides. Further, it doesn't block views, maintaining the open character of the original space.

The garage-turned-architect's-studio includes a desk, long enough for two people, additional desk space along the window wall, abundant shelving, a sitting area with a built-in L-shape sofa and flat-screen TV, and a loft bed. All the millwork was customized to maximize the use of space.

035

The new studio is unique, functional, and comfortable, with three types of wood used for flooring, wall paneling, and furniture. The use of the same material throughout creates a sense of spatial continuity, yet the different woods offer subtle color and texture variations that enrich the quality of the space.

LivingHome YB1

625 sq ft

California, United States

fuseproject and Plant Prefab, Inc.

© fuseproject and Plant Prefab, Inc.

Steve Glenn, the founder of Plant Prefab, approached fuseproject, led by Yves Behar, to design a prefab system that covers a range of consumer needs and price ranges. The first model, the LivingHome YB1, is a system that allows customization of every structure from a layout, size (400–1,500 square feet), roofline (pitched or flat roof), window size and location, and external material standpoint. The YB1 is designed to showcase the design, quality of workmanship, flexibility, and sustainability that LivingHomes is known for. It is available immediately, and upon order, it takes about four weeks for manufacturing and one day for installation with all electrical, plumbing, lighting, HVAC, and appliances built-in.

036

Modular construction is adaptable
to different site conditions, design
interests, and lifestyle preferences
thanks to its flexible features such as
module size, easy and fast assembly,
and possible relocation.

The adaptability, affordability, and sustainable elements of the YB1 system make it a standout in the market. YB1 homes are completely customizable, with a wide range of creative building configurations. Additionally, the homes can be built at any size, as the design is such that the size of the homes can range from 400 to 1,500 square feet.

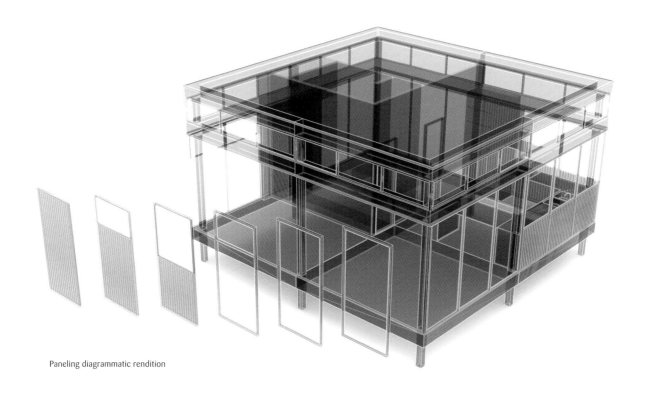

Paneling diagrammatic rendition

fuseproject and Yves Behar have been
working in affordable and efficient living
for the last few years with Ori, a robotic
furniture company that transforms junior
studios into multifunctional livable
homes. For Yves Behar, the next frontier
of design is to think of the entire home
as a product that a homeowner can
shape to their needs in terms of size,
usage, and aesthetic.

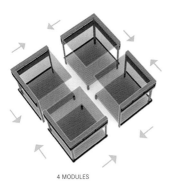

4 MODULES

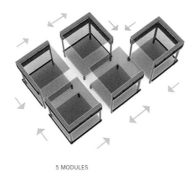

5 MODULES

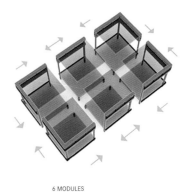

6 MODULES

Proprietary component-based building system

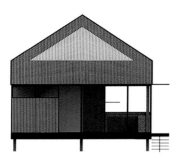

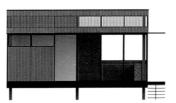

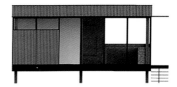

Elevation options

The design is cost-efficient and adheres to LivingHomes' high environmental efficiency standards, using materials like wood slats paneling, concrete, and stucco panels. The model options are also responsive to climate. For example, flat roofs allowing for solar panels can be incorporated, which work well in southern regions; likewise, the design of pitch roofs assimilate well in colder areas and mountain regions.

037

Walls take up space and make small spaces feel even tinier. Instead, open plans optimize the use of the available space and create a feeling of amplitude. The arrangement of furniture can be an effective tool to create different zones with no need for walls.

The owners wanted a small studio down a dirt road from their main house on a large property once used for livestock grazing. The new studio is located in its own private open space beside a 75-year-old cast-in-place concrete livestock watering trough and separated from the main house by a grove of trees. It can be used to accommodate guests or as a quiet workplace. The building has galvanized corrugated metal siding and roofing found on many old rural farm structures in Marin County and was designed as a two-story building to minimize its footprint on the land. The stepped roofs shelter distinct layers of space underneath. The outer layer contains a kitchenette, a bathroom, storage, and cozy sitting areas. The middle layer contains the circulation. The highest gabled roof shelters the final layer, which is better described as the rugged core—a two-story structure with the loft above and the living room directly below.

Marin County Studio

398 sq ft

Marin County, California, United States

Robert Nebolon Architects

Computer Generated Imagery (CGI): © Robert Nebolon Architects

The studio was designed to look like a farm out-building, a structure commonly found in rural Marin County. A small deck connects the house to the old watering trough. A large, yellow 12-foot-high glass and wood pocket door can be opened to the deck on warm evenings.

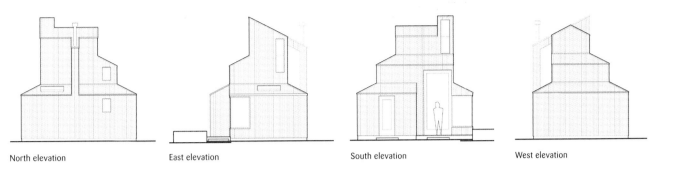

North elevation

East elevation

South elevation

West elevation

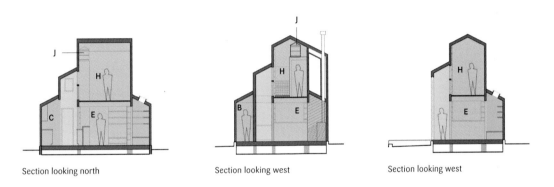

Section looking north

Section looking west

Section looking west

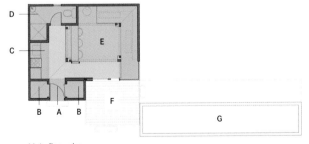

Main floor plan

Loft plan

Roof plan

A. Entry
B. Storage
C. Kitchen
D. Bathroom
E. Living area
F. Deck
G. Cattle watering trough
H. Loft
I. Open to below
J. Water tank

Marin County Studio **133**

The loft structure is left unpainted
and rustic to contrast with the refined
white-painted walls and ceilings of the
surrounding spaces

038

Space and storage are planned with dual uses. The built-in couches in the living room are also twin beds with the bedding stored in large drawers underneath. The bar serves as a dining space and also as a work area.

039

The loft is designed to be an office or art studio and is currently used as a bedroom for adventuresome guests. The recycled lumber and wood paneling are unpainted for a rustic ambiance.

040

The bed is a captain's bed—a type of bed raised for storage underneath. Colorful plastic milk crates provide storage for bedding and clothing in niches at the foot of the bed.

The loft structure consists of rustic recycled lumber and wood paneling to contrast with the white refined finishes of the surrounding spaces, to make the studio feel larger. High walls provide space for wall-hung artwork and built-in shelves provide space for books.

The corner casement window can be opened completely to create an open cantilevered corner with unobstructed views of the water-filled trough and the meadow.

The Malibu Studio is a prototypical design for a dwelling in a prominent rural and fire-prone location. With a small but efficient footprint, it treads lightly on the landscape but takes advantage of the spectacular ocean and mountain views offered by the site.

The building form began as a simple double-height studio space, partially buried in the ground to reduce its apparent height. The north side, which is the most vulnerable to winter winds and fire, is treated like a hard carapace covered with corrugated metal. Deep window reveals allow focused views of Boney Ridge. The north wall forms a wrapper that leans out to capture storage space, wraps over the roof, and extends as an overhang on the south side.

Malibu Studio

700 sq ft

Malibu, California,
United States

**Nick Roberts, AIA and
Cory Buckner, Architect**

© Nick Roberts, Chris Hall,
George Pesce

041

Glass walls open up an interior to the surrounding natural setting and valley beyond, amplifying the perception of the interior space.

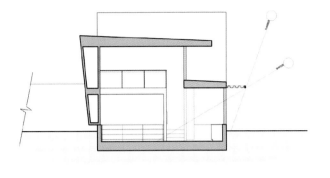

The form and color of the building are carefully selected to blend in with the slope of the hills across the valley and the color of the surrounding chaparral.

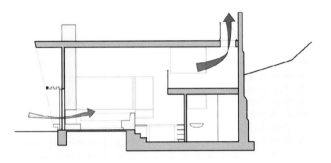

Sections

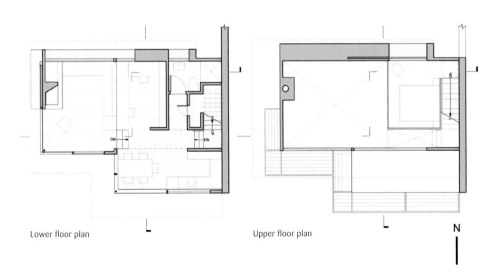

Lower floor plan

Upper floor plan

N

042

Double-height ceilings are perhaps one of the most dramatic features, creating airy and bright spaces. A loft can complete the space by adding dimension while providing room for sleeping and a view of the entire living space below.

Big panoramic windows frame the views,
making the surrounding nature part
of the house design, which embraces
beauty and sensory experience.

Shalev

400 sq ft

New York, New York,
United States

Architecture Workshop PC

© Robert Garneau

The Shalev client wanted to optimize their studio apartment that felt cluttered with an oversized dressing room and awkward sleeping area. Architecture Workshop PC transformed this tiny home into an airy and light-filled space by converting the underutilized walk-in closet into a cozy sleeping space. Sliding panels transform the apartment, offering different views, expanding and contracting the space as needed. The panels are painted the same color as the walls around them, creating continuous surfaces. When opened, they reveal generous storage throughout, whether it is a bookcase and television set or new storage under the windows, hiding radiators. In line with the optimization of space use, the top of the under-window storage serves as additional counter space.

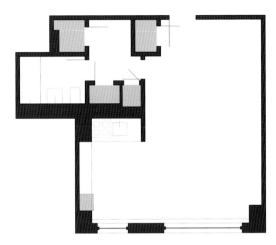

Original floor plan

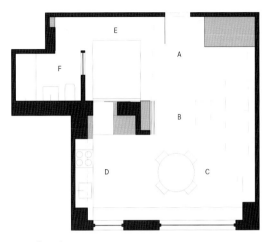

New floor plan

A. Foyer   D. Kitchen
B. Living area   E. Bedroom
C. Dining area   F. Bathroom

Access to the bathroom was moved to the side. A new frosted glass door was provided and a frosted glass panel was used to infill the original opening. The frosted glass allows for natural light to reach the dark bathroom while offering privacy.

043

Privacy is achieved by sliding
panels to provide partial or
complete enclosure as needed.

044

The sleeping area has a window into the kitchen. Sliding a wood panel creates separation or admits daylight when desired. The custom bed has a sliding headboard panel to access storage.

045

A new compact closet expands like a suitcase when needed while providing a similar capacity to the prior walk-in closet.

Despite the small size of the site, the design offers comfortable living for a family of five. Yet, it presented two important challenges: one, the configuration of the new space had to balance family life and the need for privacy, and two, given that the house only had natural light coming from the front and the back, additional lighting had to be provided from the roof. The latter was critical to bring light into the central section of the home. Working with a small space meant that the design had to focus on making every square inch usable. Every surface can become a different element: a cabinet or a fold-out table, a bookcase or a staircase, a sofa or a bed; multifunctionality at its best.

Nanluoguxiang Hutong

258 sq ft
Beijing, China

B.L.U.E. Architecture Studio

© Ruijing Photo

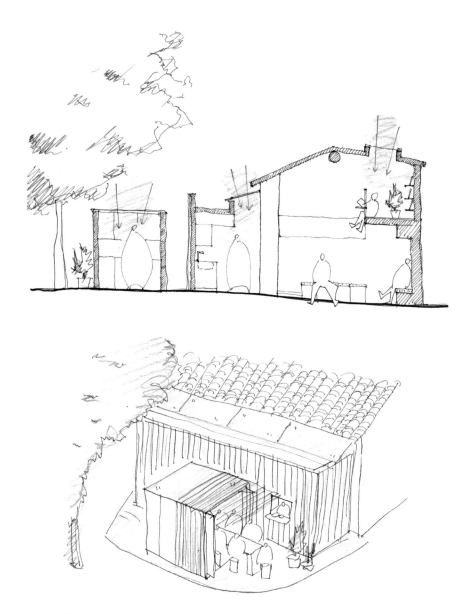

Design development sketches

Design development sketches

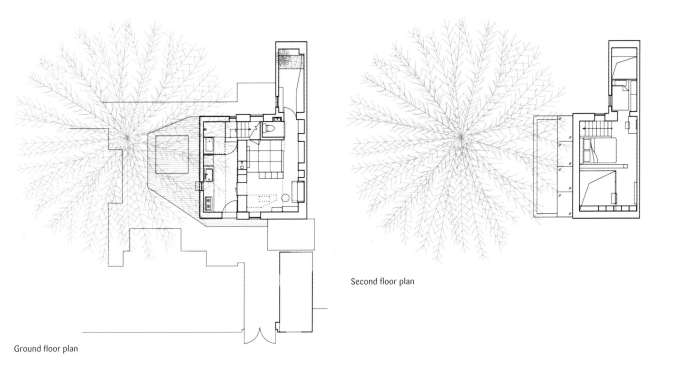

Second floor plan

Ground floor plan

Building section

046

Multifunctional furnishings and innovative storage solutions were key to the creation of a space-efficient yet comfortable living environment.

047

The main goal was to incorporate as many storage solutions as possible, including the lining of walls with shelves and cabinets, and multifunctional spaces such as the dining and living room, which doubles as a bedroom.

048

Shelves at seat height line the walls whenever possible to promote interaction among family members.

The space-saving reconfiguration of the space also takes advantage of the high ceiling to make room for a second level bathed in the light from the new skylights.

An L-shape site accommodates a home for a family of six, wedged between a masonry wall facing the street and a two-story building. The design is a tour de force displaying outstanding planning and space-saving solutions to accommodate the occupants' needs as a family and as individuals. Taking advantage of the high ceiling, a wood structure accommodates all the domestic functions, including eating, cooking, sleeping, and bathing. Because it is only half the height of the space, the top of the structure serves as additional usable space.

Dengshikou Hutong Residence

463 sq ft
Beijing, China

B.L.U.E. Architecture Studio

© Ruijing Photo

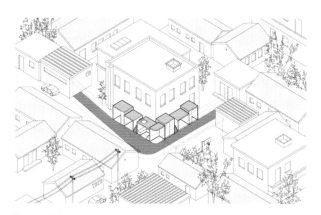

Conceptual diagram

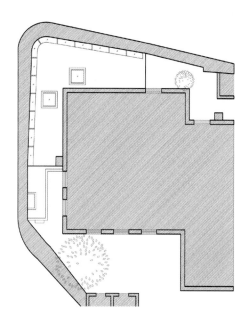

Roof plan

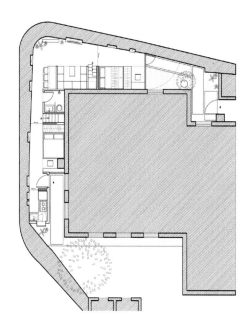

Ground floor plan

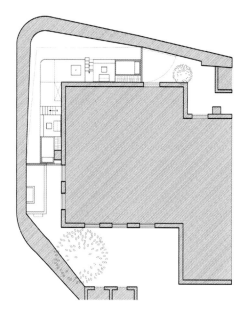

Second floor plan

170 Dengshikou Hutong Residence

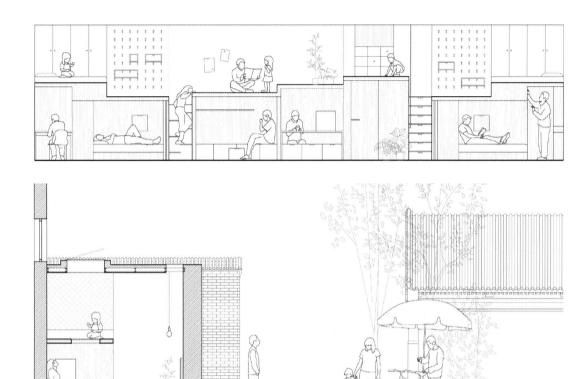

Building sections

049

The wood structure is composed of seven boxes, each dedicated to a specific use. The function of these niches determines their size and form, creating spatial variation and encouraging movement and exploration.

050

Through a cleverly thought-through track system, the boxes can expand or shrink, revealing extra storage or foldaway tables at any given time.

051

The leftover space generates
a continuous open area that
promotes interaction between family
members, while a series of sliding
panels ensures that each family
member can enjoy their own
private space.

An open space on top of the wood structure accommodates a sleeping area for the youngest of the family, a playroom, and a library.

052

The project offers endless design opportunities to explore space optimization solutions that fulfill functional requirements and satisfy the need for always useful storage.

053

Natural light, brought into the home through various skylights, is a critical element of the design, contributing to the creation of an interior space that feels larger than it is.

ADU Portland

1024 sq ft

Portland, Oregon,
United States

Webster Wilson

© Caitlin Murray

This Auxiliary Dwelling Unit (ADU) was designed as a minimalist retirement home in the backyard of the owner's daughter. While it is ultra-efficient and functional, the abundant natural light and meticulously crafted wood detailing create a warm, humane environment that expands out beyond the building envelope into the garden. The main floor is a multipurpose living area, with playful built-ins and large patio doors connecting to the outdoors. The entire second floor is a master suite with an additional sleeping loft for the grandchildren.

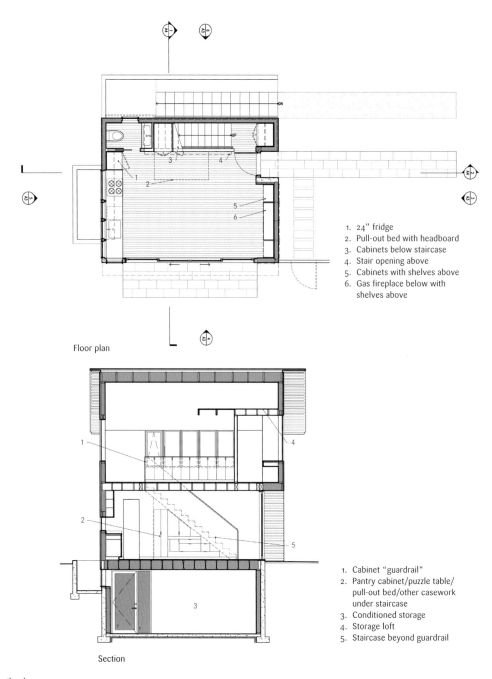

Floor plan

1. 24" fridge
2. Pull-out bed with headboard
3. Cabinets below staircase
4. Stair opening above
5. Cabinets with shelves above
6. Gas fireplace below with shelves above

Section

1. Cabinet "guardrail"
2. Pantry cabinet/puzzle table/ pull-out bed/other casework under staircase
3. Conditioned storage
4. Storage loft
5. Staircase beyond guardrail

054

This design proves that a sizable home with a minimal footprint makes for compact yet comfortable living.

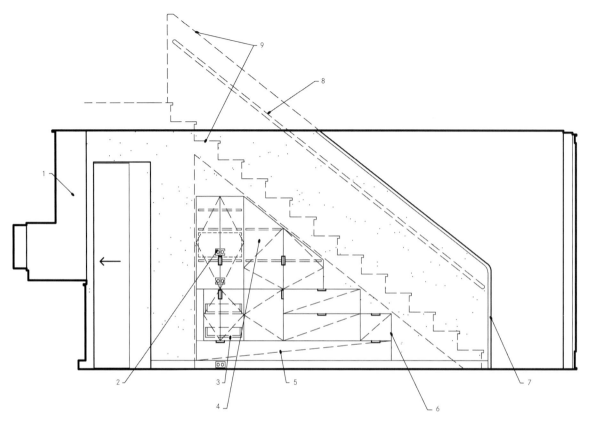

Elevation at living room cabinetry

1. Cabinet sidewall for fridge
2. Microwave/small appliance locations with outlets
3. Pantry cabinet with roller drawers
4. Solid panel cabinet
5. Twin bed pull-out "drawer" with headboard and built-in
   reading light
6. Cabinet doors flush with wallboard
7. Hardwood top rail with turned-down waterfall edge
8. Solid wood handrail
9. Staircase beyond; rail continues to second floor

055

The space underneath a staircase is often underused and hard to put to good use. It does provide, however, an ideal spot for a built-in that can combine closet space, drawers, and shelves. It also provides enough depth for a pull-out single bed.

056

Wall kitchens give homes an open and contemporary feel. They feature a single linear workspace with countertops, appliances, and cabinetry designed to make the most of small spaces. Their compact yet stylish design frees up floor area that can be enjoyed as part of an open plan living and dining area.

057

Spending money on well-crafted,
bespoke pieces of furniture is worth
the cost in the long run as they last
a lifetime.

058

Boat-inspired ideas are all about compact design solutions for reduced spaces. Ladders, hatches, and lofts, among other features, are conceived with practicality and space-saving capabilities in mind.

Quatre Septembre Apartment

926 sq ft
Paris, France

Alia Bengana

© C. Baechtold, V. Vincenzo

When the client, a photojournalist, bought the apartment, it was unfit for habitation. A poorly lit, narrow, winding entry hall led to a living room that opened onto a kitchen and then onto a bedroom and a bathroom. He wanted a simple space, as open as possible with areas spreading into one another. The new layout had to include an additional bedroom and a multifunctional living area that could be used as a living room, dining room, kitchen, and office. The apartment had character, but the low ceilings and load-bearing walls connecting all the rooms limited the redesign options. The design makes the most of the home's potential through smart floor planning to improve the connection between areas and through transformable furnishings that add convenience and functionality.

059

This living area can fulfill the functions of a kitchen and dining room thanks to a system of retractable furniture.

060

The kitchen's backsplash can fold out open to visually connect the entire home and allow natural light from the living area into the middle of the apartment.

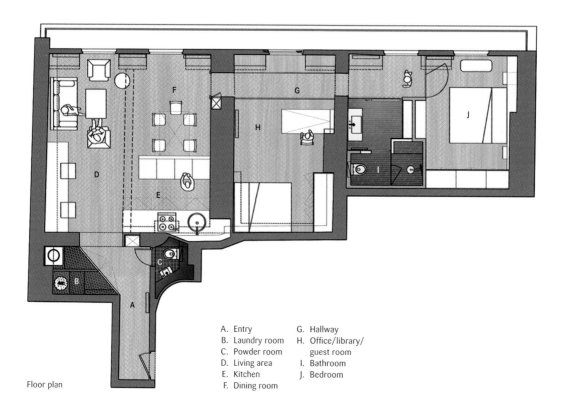

A. Entry
B. Laundry room
C. Powder room
D. Living area
E. Kitchen
F. Dining room
G. Hallway
H. Office/library/
   guest room
I. Bathroom
J. Bedroom

Floor plan

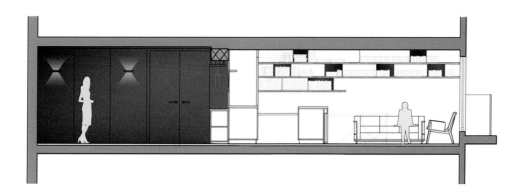

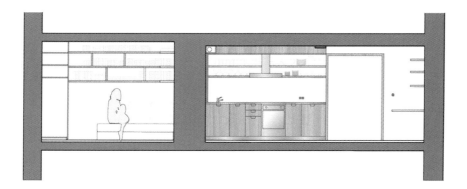

Sections

061

The design emphasizes the contrast between the dark entry hall and the bright living area. A funneling effect is achieved by building a closet diagonally in the hallway. It conceals the laundry room and the utility closet.

062

Along the window wall, a storage bench doubles as a step to facilitate access to the balcony.

063

In the guest bedroom, which doubles as a library, a desk folds away against the wall when not needed to free space up.

UWS Apartment

985 sq ft

New York, New York,
United States

Format Architecture Office

© Nick Glimenakis

This gut renovated apartment in a historic Gothic Revival co-op on Riverside Drive leverages a mixture of clean lines and prewar-inspired details to celebrate the eclectic tastes of its owner. The primary goals for the project were to create flexible connections between spaces, enhance access to natural light, and maximize storage. A home office adjacent to the living room doubles as a guest room; an added powder room and a fully reconfigured kitchen with expanded storage space increase flexibility.

Organized around a single circulation spine, each daylit room acts as a patchwork of color and texture stitched together by a thickened threshold detail between each space, expressed throughout in rich anigre wood.

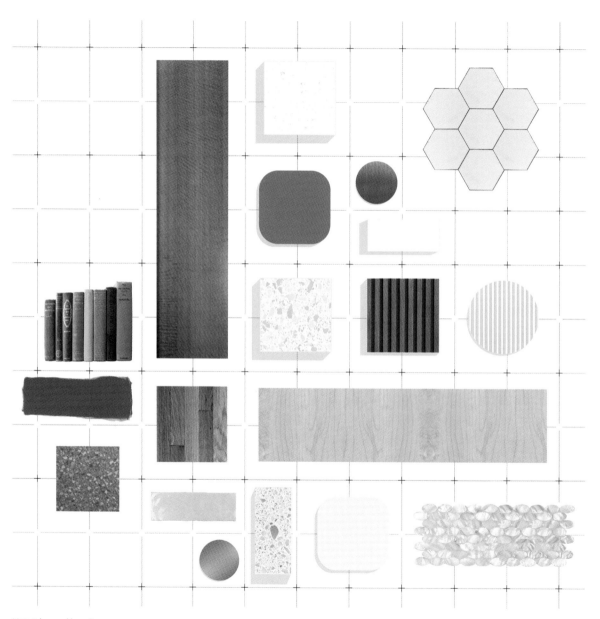

Materials mood board

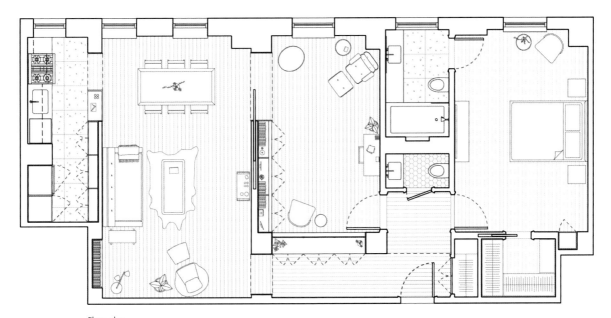

Floor plan

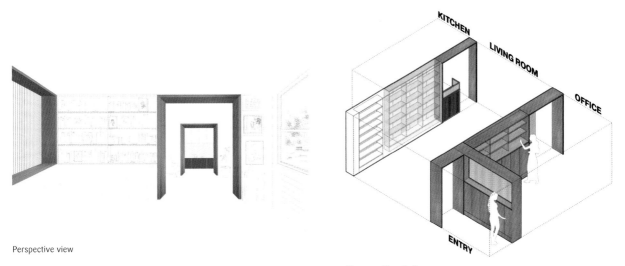

Perspective view

Storage millwork diagram

064

Pocket doors are particularly well suited where floor space is at a premium. They disappear into doorways, turning two or more contiguous rooms into one large seamless space.

065

Frosted glass is perhaps the most commonly used in windows and doors to let light through while obscuring the view. Among other options are tinted, glue-chip, and fluted glass, as shown in the images above.

Large thresholds between public spaces celebrate transitions and become extensions of different wood-clad storage solutions that complement the myriad needs of a small domestic space.

Ribbed glass dividers between the entry hallway and office, coupled with glass transoms above each doorway, pull natural light deeper into the apartment.

066

Color accents don't necessarily overwhelm small spaces or make them feel cramped. When used moderately, they add personality and visual interest.

Semi-Nary

400 sq ft

New York, New York,
United States

Architecture Workshop PC

© Robert Garneau

Semi-Nary is a compact loft apartment located in the former home of the New York Theological Seminary. The clients wanted a place that, despite its reduced dimensions, could comfortably accommodate overnight guests. The place also had to be suitable for entertaining. Abundant storage, flexible use of space, tall ceiling height, and generous natural lighting are some of the highlights of this tiny apartment design, demonstrating that functionality and not extra space is key for comfortable living. Transformable furnishings adapt the space to different situations. A height-adjustable table provides a multifunctional work surface and expands to seat 10. The design is complete with an entertainment cabinet with a fireplace, and a hidden hydraulic TV behind that anchors the tall space while the upper wall is used for projection.

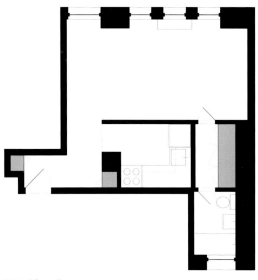

Original floor plan

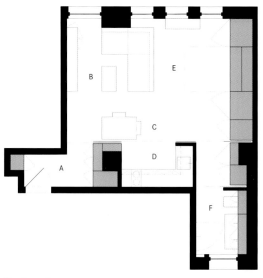

New floor plan

A. Foyer   D. Kitchen
B. Living area   E. Sleeping area
C. Dining area   F. Bathroom

067

Sliding partitions allow the kitchen, bathroom, and foyer to be closed off from the main space, creating a more intimate quiet area.

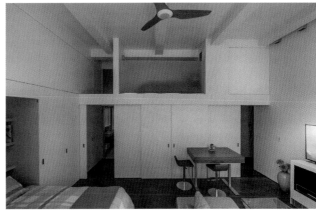

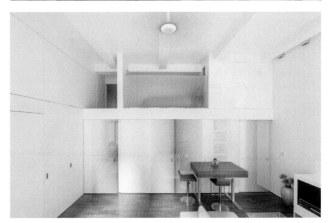

068

The compartmentalization of spaces that serve different functions isn't permanent. This allows flexible use of the space, combining the different areas into one single open space, very convenient for entertaining, or separating them to create smaller private areas.

The design takes advantage of the apartment's 14-foot-ceiling height to make room for a sleeping loft above the kitchen, while everyday sleeping is provided with a wall bed in the main space.

The apartment features extensive
custom cabinetry that includes a
large wall of closets with a Murphy
bed and a home office.

069

The bathroom features a curbless shower with an inconspicuous glass door that bisects a double sink, allowing two people to use the bathroom independently. An oversized mirror cabinet expands the appearance of the room while custom light cylinders float in the lofted space overhead.

Clinton Hill Loft

920 sq ft

Brooklyn, New York,
United States

**Dean Works
Architecture + Design**

© Daniel Salemi

The design for this studio loft in a former factory building in Brooklyn started with the clients' Baltic-birch plywood table, which they had designed and built before the project began. The clients, of studio GLAM, hired Brandon Dean, of Dean Works Architecture + Design, to help design a new kitchen and bedroom that took inspiration from the clean details, material, and proportions of the original table. The new custom closets, steel frame sliding-glass doors, and cabinetry were designed to slip into the loft space neatly, maintain the industrial character, and provide much-needed storage for the couple's growing collection of art, records, ceramics, books, and dog toys. Dean worked closely with the clients to source unique lighting fixtures, appliances, and materials, and designed the kitchen to be highly functional yet fantastic for entertaining.

The inserted plywood structure with walls, cabinets, and doorways organizes the loft. This design solution effectively fulfills two goals: add storage and separate the bedroom from the rest of the home while maintaining the loft feel.

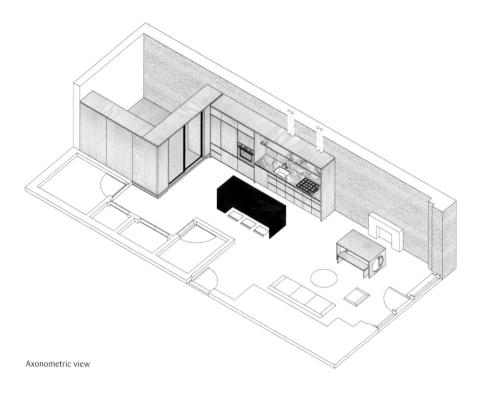

Axonometric view

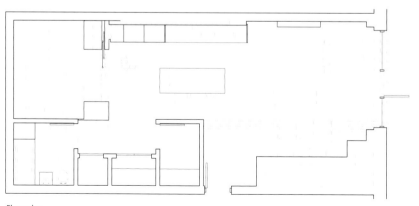

Floor plan

070

Built-ins can provide a variety of closed and open storage and countertops, making the most of the available space.

071

Not only are built-ins very practical, but they can be designed to fit a specific style using the materials and finishes of one's choice.

072

Translucent surfaces allow light through and, at the same time, block the view to give privacy. They are the ideal room divider to preserve an open feel.

073

With no need for door jambs or headers, pocket doors are a clean and stylish design feature that can be used in extra-wide openings, connecting adjacent rooms seamlessly.

074

Wall-mounted cabinets and shelves seem less obtrusive and bulky than their freestanding counterparts because we can see the floor extending underneath them. This lightweight-looking furniture type is ideal for rooms of limited dimensions where we don't want to create a cramped feel.

Fujigaoka M

689 sq ft

Kanagawa, Japan

Sinato

© Toshiyuki Yano

The renovation of a small apartment was aimed at creating a living space as open as possible, but with various areas of different functions. The solution is an L-shape wooden structure that generates different areas. Its central position allows it to free up the space along two walls with windows. This contributes to the apartment's open character, while the central structure offers various storage and seating solutions. The wood makes the apartment homely and inviting.

075

The L-shape wooden structure is conceived as a multifunctional large piece of furniture. As such, it is separate from the preexisting concrete and plaster shell of the apartment.

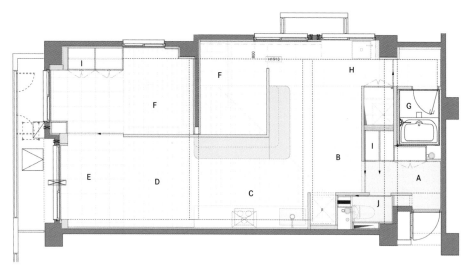

Floor plan

A. Entry
B. Living area
C. Kitchen
D. Dining area
E. Area for relaxation

F. Bedroom
G. Bathroom
H. Washroom
I. Storage
J. Toilet room

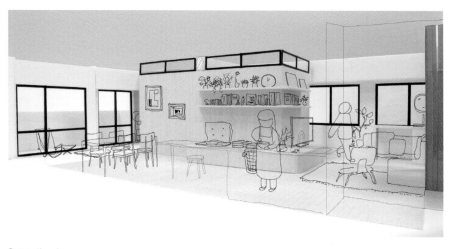

Perspective view

The wood structure extends along the longitudinal axis of the apartment to become a wall separating the bedroom from the dining and relaxation areas.

076

Additional pieces of furniture along the perimeter of the apartment offer specific support for each of the functions of the household, such as the kitchen cooking area and the vanity.

The long wooden wall extending from the central structure emphasizes the apartment's longitudinal axis, offering minimal obstruction to light from the south wall.

The bedroom faces a fully glazed wall, benefiting from abundant light and a sense of openness. Like any other area in the apartment, the bedroom is not conceived as a room, but as a space generated by the wooden structure.

Sonoma weeHouse®

970 sq ft (640 main +
330 guest)
Sonoma, California,
United States

Alchemy Architects

© Alchemy Architects

Designed in Minnesota, built in Oregon, and delivered to the client
in California, Alchemy's Sonoma weeHouse® received a "2018
Small Projects Award" from a jury of architects chosen by the
American Institute of Architects (AIA) based in Washington,
DC. In reference to the Small Projects category, the AIA website
mentioned: "A small project can make a big impact, and a single
design element can set the tone for large projects."

The Sonoma weeHouse® is a small, ultraminimal, prefabricated
home designed by Geoffrey C. Warner, FAIA and customized in
collaboration with the client. The project is composed of two
open-sided prefabricated boxes set on concrete plinths nestled
on the edge of gnarled oaks in the hills outside of Santa Rosa,
California. The two structures were shipped essentially complete.

077

Sonoma weeHouse® is conceived as two windows taking in the views of the breathtaking natural surroundings. The reduced dimensions of the interiors are hardly an issue.

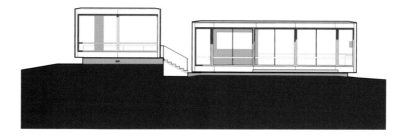

Elevation

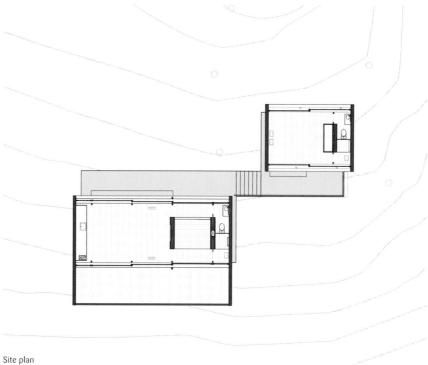

Site plan

Both structures feature steel frames, 9-foot-tall sliding-glass walls, ipe interiors, and custom oiled oak doors on stock cabinetry. They are both sided in corrugated weathering steel, and sited to take advantage of the dramatic, sweeping views.

For shipping, the main structure, the largest of the two, was designed as two modules: a 16' × 40' main box, and a 10' × 40' porch.

078

The floor-to-ceiling sliding-glass doors minimize the interior-exterior boundary, making the landscape as much part of the home as the home is part of the landscape.

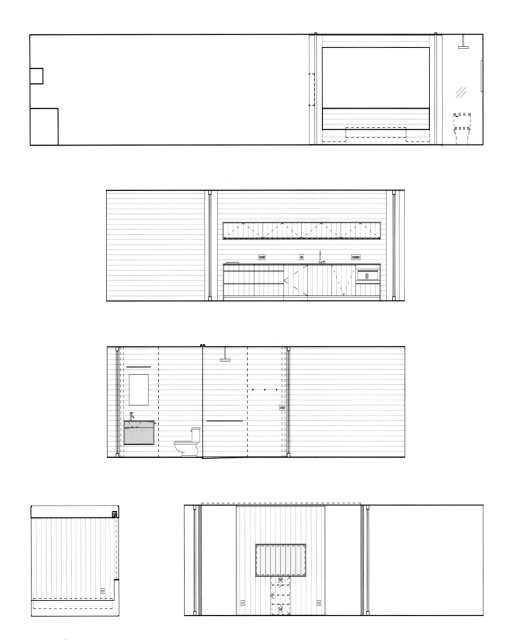

Interior elevations

079

The open character of the Sonoma weeHouse® makes up for the reduced dimensions of the modules.

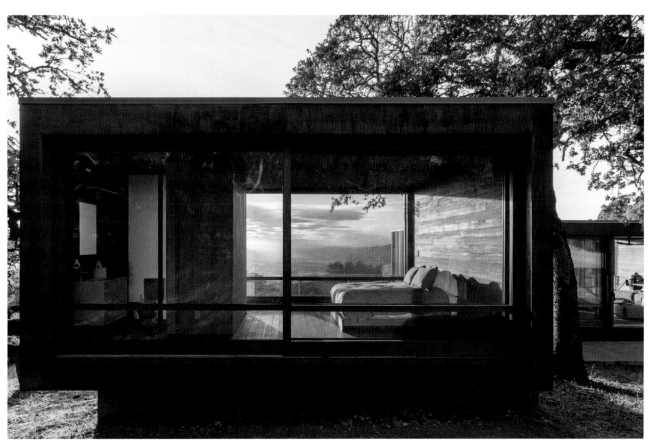

The transparency of the house is one of the best features of the house. Its glass walls open up the interior to the surrounding landscape, allowing nature to be part of the home.

080

When the sun goes down, Sonoma
weeHouse® adopts another
dimension. With its generous
fenestration, the house glows
like a lantern.

Apartment V01

850 sq ft
Sofia, Bulgaria

dontDIY

© Asen Emilov

Maximizing natural lighting and creating a comfortable living
environment were the primary goals in the redesign of this
apartment. Various areas were combined to maximize the use
of space, creating a comfortable home while eliminating the
original crowded feel and bringing in abundant natural light.
The vestibule was enlarged at the expense of a utilities room,
and the existing kitchen was transformed into a dressing room.
The storage requirement was satisfied by creative built-ins and
freestanding units that, at the same time, guide the circulation
through the apartment. A herringbone flooring and an eclectic
furnishing selection spice up the minimalistic design, giving the
old apartment a new life full of character.

081

The fireplace is integrated into a full-height wall cabinet, which also contains the refrigerator and the air-conditioning unit. Painted white to match the walls, it contributes to the creation of an unencumbered layout.

The plywood wall kitchen can be concealed behind a retractable screen. The fireplace, refrigerator, and air-conditioning unit are integrated into the various built-ins.

082

The new kitchen, made of plywood built-ins, is attuned to the bookcase in the living area. When not in use, it can disappear behind sliding panels, adding to the simple yet inviting look of the apartment.

083

A brightly colored freestanding
bookshelf is made to stand out,
as opposed to a wall of integrated
cabinets with their fronts finished in
the same color as the walls around
them to make them disappear.

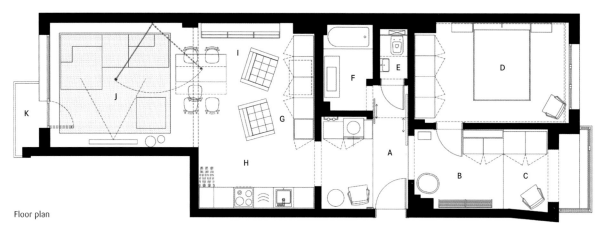

Floor plan

A. Vestibule
B. Boudoir
C. Yoga/deck
D. Bedroom
E. Toilet room
F. Bathroom
G. Seating area
H. Concealed kitchen
I. Workspace/
   dining area
J. TV area
K. Balcony

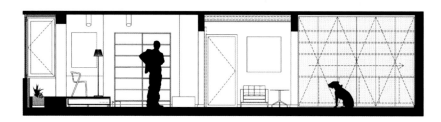

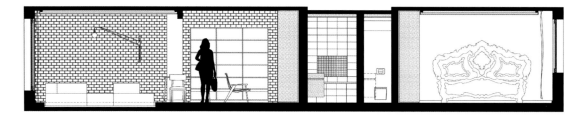

Sections

084

Both the bedroom and the bathroom are minimal, sparsely furnished, and equipped with just what is essential.

The 3-in-1 Room

110 sq ft

Nashville, Tennessee,
United States

New Frontier Design

© David Latimer

A 9' × 12' Accessory Dwelling Unit room above a garage was
turned into a makeup/photo studio, guest room, and personal
storage room. To achieve these goals, the New Frontier Design
team put into practice its expertise in maximizing space, whether
it is by transforming the footprint of a single room or changing the
layout of an entire home. The makeover of the room is custom
designed, tailored to the needs of the client. Given the space
limitations of the room, fitting a full guest room was unviable, but
a Murphy bed, on the other hand, would fulfill the need for a guest
room and free up floor space when the Murphy bed is folded away
to use the room as a makeup/photo studio. Abundant storage was
provided as required, and the design team exceeded the client's
expectations, making the room feel large and spacious.

085

The success of this makeover lies in
multifunctionality. A single piece of
cabinetry can turn the small room
into a guest room and a makeup/
photo studio.

086

Storage is all about organization.
A variety of storage options will
help get clutter out of sight.

087

The built-in cabinet can expand, transforming the room into a walk-in closet.

Levent House

840 sq ft
Istanbul, Turkey

COA Mimarlik

© Alt Kat Photography

The apartment was designed for a newly married couple. It was important for the designers to understand the design taste, needs, and lifestyles of the users of the apartment, both as a couple and as individuals. To better address each of the requirements, the designers encouraged their clients to engage in the design process. The apartment's original conditions presented a jigsaw layout of small rooms, corridors, and doors that created a confined atmosphere. Opening up the space was key to provide the clients with their requirements for their new home: a living space filled with light, functional, and evocative of their vibrant personalities.

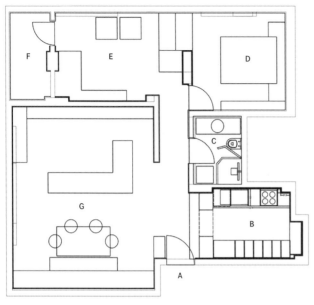

Floor plan

A. Entrance
B. Kitchen
C. Bathroom
D. Bedroom
E. Office
F. Balcony
G. Living room

088

The design of the bookshelf in the living room is a collaborative effort between the clients and the designers. The lower cabinets and the vertical white structures are fixed, while the shelves and white boxes can change position.

With minimal partitions and doors only where they are needed, the apartment's different areas flow easily into each other.

089

Open shelving lines walls and passageways. Painted white, it blends with the walls and ceiling to become a neutral backdrop for items on display.

090

Each room is decorated with the same shelving concept but with different designs, creating different stimulating environments but with a consistent aesthetic.

The bathroom design is a variation on the geometric theme that dominates the entire apartment. The all-white color scheme, which creates a clean look and calming atmosphere for the small bathroom, is only disrupted by the subtle off-white and green flooring pattern.

In the heart of urban San Francisco, a multifunctional loft designed by Peter Suen and Charles Irby transforms a small condo into a dynamic space. Custom designed and prefabricated, this project combines a guest bed, dining room, full-size closet, spacious bedroom, and dynamic work area into one compact loft. Rather than relying on kinetic components, this project instead focuses on a deliberate static configuration that harmonizes eating, working, organizing, and sleeping functions. All of the concrete panels, wood slats, metalwork, and custom cabinetry were prefabricated in Oakland, California, and reassembled on-site in San Francisco.

Domino Loft

500 sq ft

San Francisco, California, United States

Fifth Arch & ICOSA Design

© Brian Flaherty

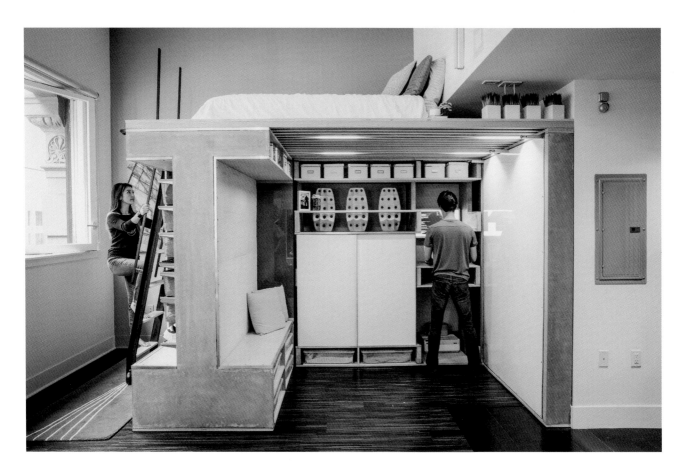

091

One major problem for tiny spaces is to decide on the right furnishings. Multifunctional furniture is a space saver. It optimizes the space available by adapting it to different uses.

092

One of the principal advantages of prefabrication is that construction generally takes place in workshops or factories. Then the parts are shipped to the site, where they are assembled. This means shorter on-site construction time and minimal construction waste.

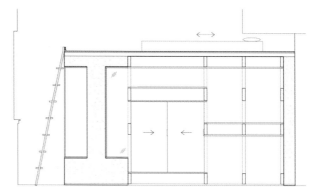

Interior elevation

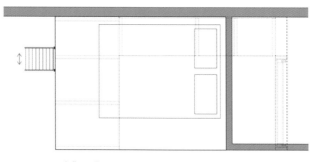

Loft floor plan

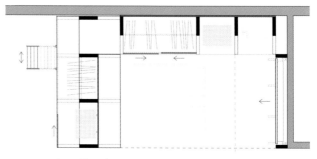

Lower floor plan

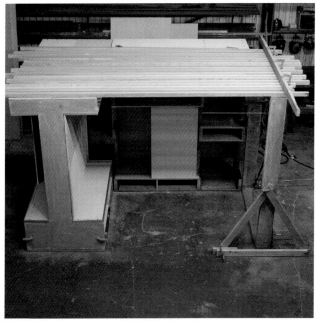

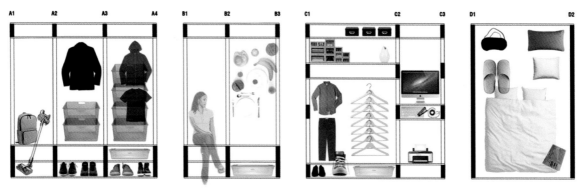

Unfolded cabinet elevation diagrams

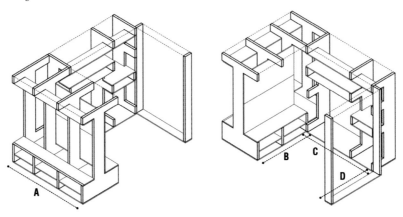

Millwork diagrams

093

Tiny spaces promote functional design solutions that optimize the use of space without sacrificing comfort. Creative solutions can also make interiors more visually appealing, adding a unique character and value to the property.

The brief for the redesign of a space called for a comfortable living place and an attractive work environment suitable to accommodate meetings with clients. The challenge the architect faced was to incorporate all the functions into a limited area. Further, the entire place had to be safe for a six-year-old boy, who would also have his own "hiding place." The design resulted in a freestanding structure made of oriented strand board (OSB) with mobile parts. The structure provides for all the functions of a home and workspace, including a wall kitchen, an office, and a sleeping loft. This design solution concentrates these functions along one wall of the studio, freeing up the rest of the space.

Brandburg Home and Studio

398 sq ft
Poznań, Poland

mode:lina

© Patryk Lewinski

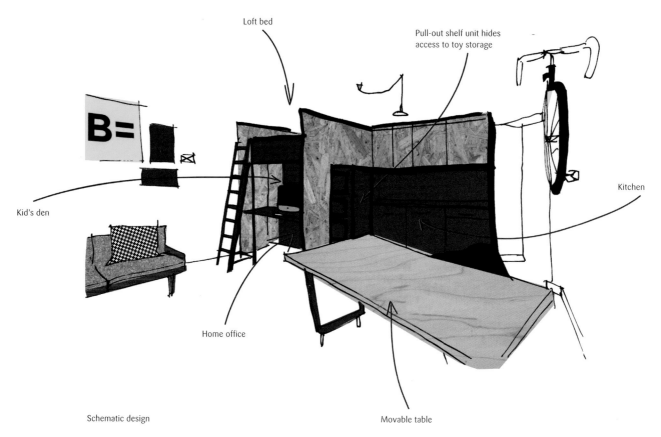

Loft bed

Pull-out shelf unit hides
access to toy storage

Kitchen

Kid's den

Home office

Movable table

Schematic design

094

The architect designed a plywood
box that integrates a kitchen, an
office, a loft bed, and a cleverly
concealed "hiding room" for a
young boy. There is also a "secret"
base that works as a toy box just
behind a movable shelf unit.

095

Small spaces offer endless design possibilities, demonstrating that functionality and personality are not reserved for larger-size spaces.

096

Numerous shelves, drawers, and cabinets are carefully integrated into the design of the black wooden box, freeing up floor space, hence creating a comfortable and roomy living and work environment.

The transformative interior renovation of Bed-Stuy Loft includes a restrained design that incorporates unfinished rough materials and muted blocks of color into the existing open-plan apartment located in a former industrial space. New architectural elements, including exposed steel, raw plywood, and expanded mesh screens, both conceal and reveal areas throughout, creating a series of distinct spaces for living, working, and sleeping. Their architectural intervention either keeps an intimate gap that mimics the outline of the column or hugs it. Inspired by the contrast between minimalist geometries and rough materials, these adjacencies of existing and new elements preserve the clean, light, continuous environment and maximize usable space without appearing overly refined.

Bed-Stuy Loft

750 sq ft

Brooklyn, New York,
United States

New Affiliates

© Michael Vahrenwald/Esto

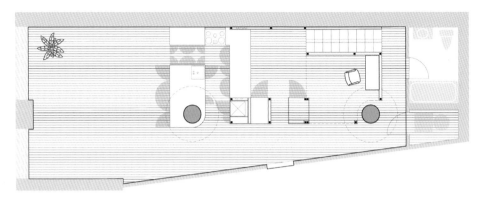

Loft level floor plan

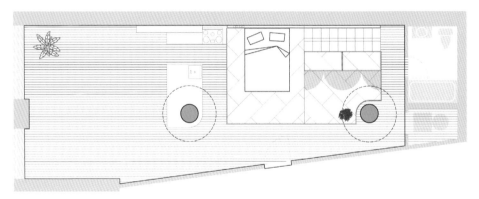

Main floor plan

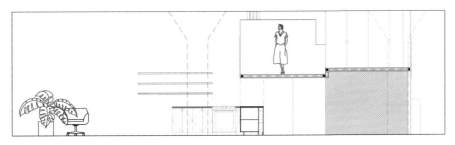

Section

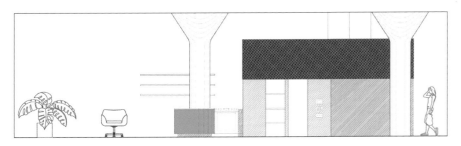

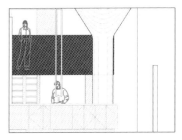

Elevations

The added elements playfully interact with two large existing columns positioned near the edge of the space, which serve as a terminating boundary for the design.

097

Avoiding tall furniture and partitions that extend to the ceiling maintains spatial continuity.

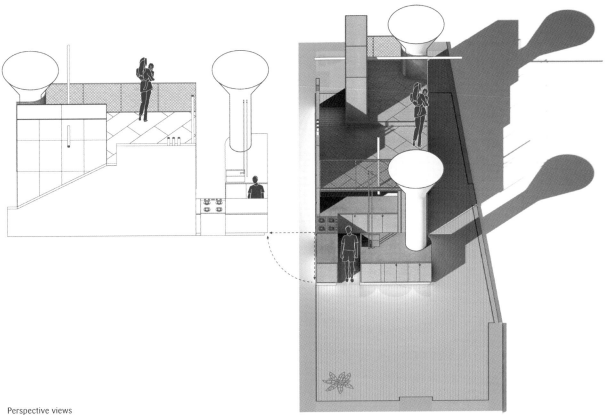

Perspective views

098

Light colors enhance spatial continuity and allow rooms to breathe. Bold colors, in the darker range, can be used sparsely to anchor contiguous areas. These two design tricks combined work well in tiny spaces to heighten the sense of space.

099

Glossy—or specular—surfaces reflect light evenly, whereas matte finishes reflect scattered light in space. When selecting colors, it is critical to choose finishes accordingly to achieve the desired effect.

The heavy interior walls are punctuated by large apertures framing curated views and bringing light from the front window wall to the back of the loft space.

Notable details include hand-selected
plywood with a distinct gradient pattern
that wraps the interior walls of the
750-square-foot interior space, carrying
into the custom-designed kitchen that
also features green lacquered kitchen
island cabinets and bright copper pipes.

100

Materials and finishes are crucial in the creation of a determined atmosphere. Materials that are reflective, transparent, or translucent create a feel of airiness and openness, qualities that are much sought after in the design of tiny spaces.

A lofted sleeping area is bounded by a floating, perforated, white metal enclosure that visually separates and connects the two distinct levels by providing privacy from oblique angles and transparency from head-on, and staggering floor heights distinguish between study/sleeping areas and guest/changing areas for homeowner and guest.

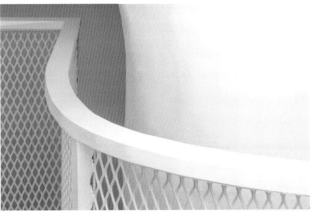

The project involved an extensive renovation of an old apartment in disrepair. While work had to be done around preexisting structural walls, an open layout and the provision for space-efficient storage provide for clutter-free and comfortable living despite the apartment's small proportions. Two major wooden boxes, serving different functions, were inserted into the exiting space, emphasizing the distinction between old and new. With the existing walls and ceiling painted white, the new wooden boxes redefine spaces and give the old apartment new life.

Fermi

753 sq ft
Turin, Italy

BLAarchitettura

© Beppe Giardino

101

The kitchen and dining area are combined in a millwork unit occupying a corner of the apartment. The kitchen concentrates high-density storage under a raised floor and compact equipment. Surrounded on two sides by the elevated kitchen and lined with cabinets along a third side, the dining area is furnished with banquettes to maximize seating.

102

Storage was designed for space efficiency through high-quality millwork, including drawers, pull-out cabinets, trapdoors, and an extendable dining table.

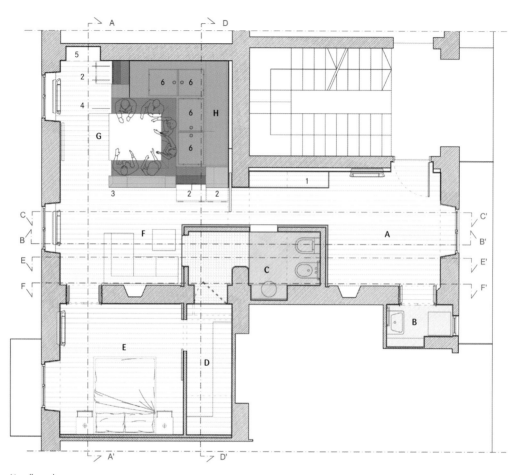

New floor plan

A. Entry/studio	1. Storage
B. Laundry room	2. Drawer
C. Bathroom	3. TV unit
D. Dressing room	4. Banquette
E. Bedroom	5. Push-and-pull door
F. Living area	6. Floor hatch
G. Dining area	
H. Kitchen	

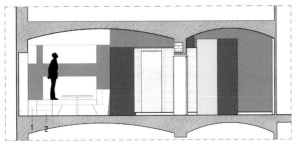

Section A

1. Push-and-pull door
2. Storage

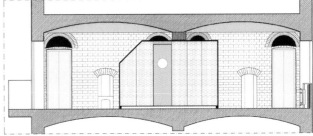

Section C

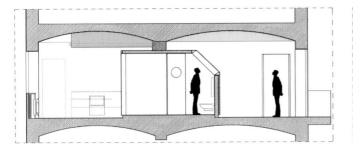

Section B

Section D

1. Floor hatch
2. Drawer

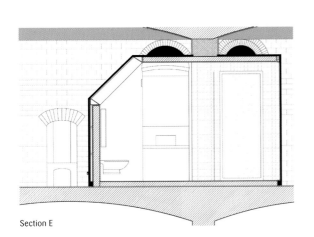

Section E

103

The bathroom is one of two inserted wooden structures. It occupies a central position in the apartment, articulating the entry, the living/dining/kitchen area, and the bedroom.

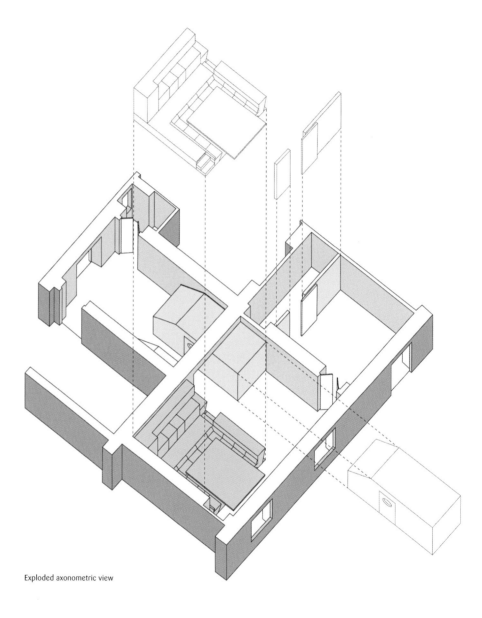

Exploded axonometric view

In the living area, two steps lead to the kitchen in an analogy to a ship's main deck.

104

The side of the bathroom's enclosure facing the living area has a frosted glass pane. This makes the wood insertion less obtrusive, and the bathroom's interior feel airier and more spacious.

An existing masonry wall revealed during the demolition work was painted over in white like the rest of the existing walls and ceilings. Its heavily textured quality adds visual interest while highlighting the contrast between preexisting and new.

Focus on high-quality millwork and careful material selection creates a living space with a distinct character adapted to the needs and personality of the apartment's owner.

105

Sliding doors promote fluid circulation from one space to the next. They work great in tiny spaces as they require less floor area than swing doors.

Shifting Nests

269 sq ft

Vancouver, British Columbia,
Canada

**Jerry Liu and Jesse Basran/
Bla Design Group**

© Renderings: Bla Design Group

Shifting Nests is a new local nonprofit initiative that aims to relieve financial pressure on young professionals who want to live, work, and eventually own a home in Vancouver. Each Nest utilizes a combination of micro-home housing typology and hydroponic systems to maximize the potential of these existing community gardens. Nests are mass prefabricated, and each consists linearly of twenty sectional frames; inhabitants can customize their home according to their individual needs and the different functions these frames provide. Nests are entirely off-grid and energy independent. This initiative allows young professional couples to double their monthly savings, making it possible for them to save a down payment for a home in half the time.

The proposed farming method utilizes
a vertical hydroponic system. This
method is ten times more space efficient
than traditional methods and is less
dependent on seasons. It produces up to
ten times the yield of the existing method.

The land use of an existing 16,000-square-foot site is currently recreational and is a community garden. By introducing Nests to the site, the land use is converted into a combined mid-density residential and recreational use. This improves the value of the site to the community.

Vancouver, British Columbia, Canada

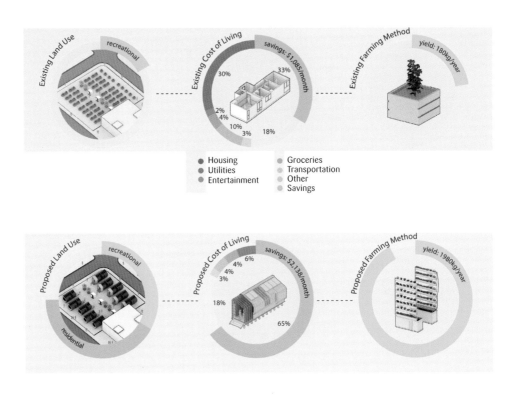

Existing Land Use — recreational

Existing Cost of Living — savings: $1,085/month
30%, 33%, 2%, 4%, 10%, 3%, 18%

Existing Farming Method — yield: 180kg/year

- ● Housing
- ● Utilities
- ● Entertainment
- ● Groceries
- ● Transportation
- ● Other
- ● Savings

Proposed Land Use — recreational, residential

Proposed Cost of Living — savings: $2,138/month
4%, 6%, 4%, 3%, 18%, 65%

Proposed Farming Method — yield: 1980kg/year

106

Despite their reduced dimensions, the Nests ensure comfortable living. The Nests are elevated from the ground to prevent heat loss, and the crawl space underneath makes room for service and mechanical units such as batteries, water reservoirs, and long-term storage spaces.

Form of Frame

The main structural frames are manufactured with sectional variations that include bay extensions, which create larger interior spaces with the same floor area. These bays can be used as seating or countertop extensions.

Modular Furniture

A series of modular plywood cubes are custom ordered for each Nest. These cubes are 0.5m X 0.5m X 0.5m in size and, depending on how the user stacks them, can provide multiple functions such as seating, countertop, bed, and storage spaces.

Section A   Unit: mm

air ventilation

Section B   Unit: mm

107

Nest occupants can customize the linear programmatic layout to suit their needs. For example, they can have living and dining in one space, as shown in Iteration 1, or they can have these functions separated with a bedroom as indicated in Iteration 2.

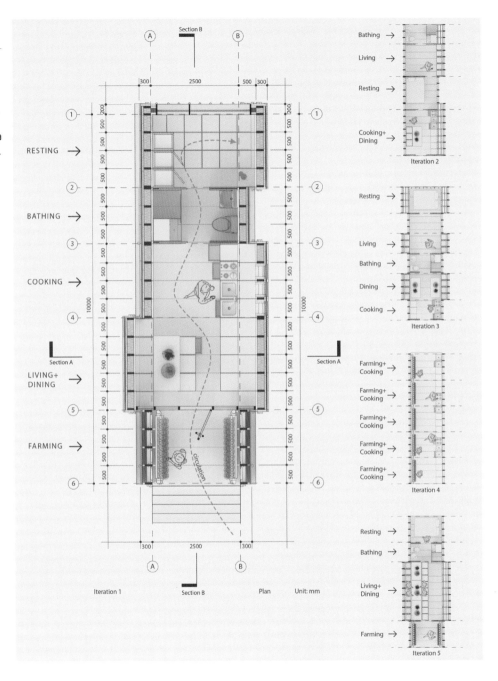

RESTING →

BATHING →

COOKING →

LIVING+ DINING →

FARMING →

Section A

Section A

Section B

Section B

Iteration 1

Plan   Unit: mm

Iteration 2
- Bathing →
- Living →
- Resting →
- Cooking+ Dining →

Iteration 3
- Resting →
- Living →
- Bathing →
- Dining →
- Cooking →

Iteration 4
- Farming+ Cooking →
- Farming+ Cooking →
- Farming+ Cooking →
- Farming+ Cooking →
- Farming+ Cooking →

Iteration 5
- Resting →
- Bathing →
- Living+ Dining →
- Farming →

circulation

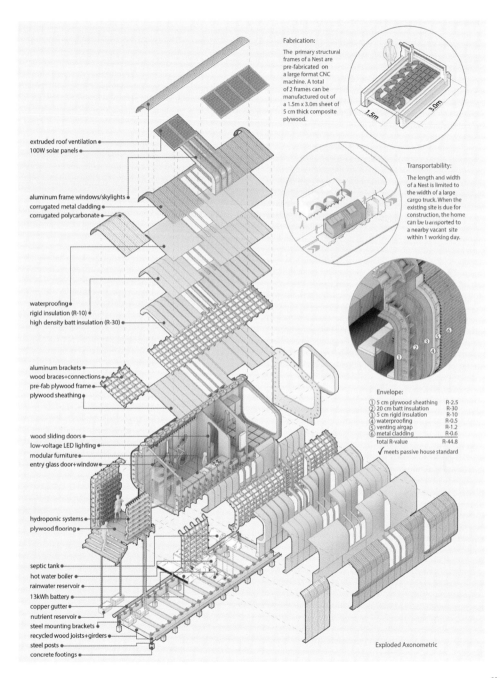

Fabrication:

The primary structural frames of a Nest are pre-fabricated on a large format CNC machine. A total of 2 frames can be manufactured out of a 1.5m x 3.0m sheet of 5 cm thick composite plywood.

1.5m
3.0m

Transportability:

The length and width of a Nest is limited to the width of a large cargo truck. When the existing site is due for construction, the home can be transported to a nearby vacant site within 1 working day.

extruded roof ventilation
100W solar panels

aluminum frame windows/skylights
corrugated metal cladding
corrugated polycarbonate

waterproofing
rigid insulation (R-10)
high density batt insulation (R-30)

aluminum brackets
wood braces+connections
pre-fab plywood frame
plywood sheathing

wood sliding doors
low-voltage LED lighting
modular furniture
entry glass door+window

hydroponic systems
plywood flooring

septic tank
hot water boiler
rainwater reservoir
13kWh battery
copper gutter
nutrient reservoir
steel mounting brackets
recycled wood joists+girders
steel posts
concrete footings

Envelope:

① 5 cm plywood sheathing	R-2.5
② 20 cm batt insulation	R-30
③ 5 cm rigid insulation	R-10
④ waterproofing	R-0.5
⑤ venting airgap	R-1.2
⑥ metal cladding	R-0.6
total R-value	R-44.8

√ meets passive house standard

Exploded Axonometric

108

Air is vented both horizontally and vertically through the Nests, entering from the front where the plants grow and exiting through the operable skylights, roof vents, and the large window at the rear.

Flat 8

550 sq ft
Hong Kong, SAR China

Design Eight Five Two

© Hazel Yuen Fun

For Flat 8, the client's brief was simple: to create a home as large as space and functions would allow. Based on these premises, the design focuses on optimizing natural lighting to create an open and airy feel and providing generous and functional storage. The design solution to optimize the use of space is a flexible layout. The apartment includes a living area and a bedroom. They can either be seamlessly connected to create an ample open space filled with light or can be separated from each other to satisfy privacy needs.

109

To maximize the use of space, the design explores the storage possibilities on the horizontal and vertical planes. A raised platform taking up half the apartment's area provides generous storage. The platform then extends vertically along one wall to create a desk and bookshelves.

110

In the living area, an extendable table to accommodate family gatherings and various large pull-out drawers are some of the key design features to make efficient use of space.

111

The platform also serves to
demarcate areas of different
functions, demonstrating that
walls are not the only dividers.

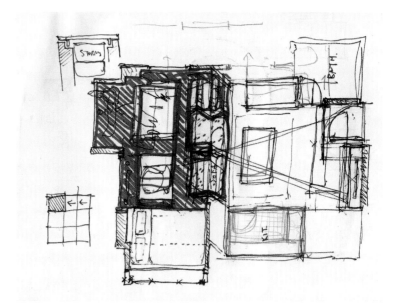

Conceptual design sketch

Floor plan

112

Movable partitions and oversize
doors pair up with various creative
storage solutions to provide
the space with a clutter-free,
comfortable atmosphere.

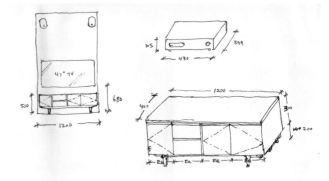

Wall unit design sketches

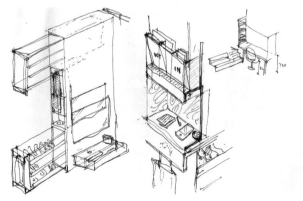

Pull-out drawers design sketches

Dutchess County Studio

750 sq ft

Amenia, New York,
United States

GRT Architects

© Ithai Schori

GRT Architects designed a studio for Manhattanites considering a move. Living and working in a large city inevitably involves conversations about leaving it. The clients raised their children in the Frank Lloyd Wright-planned Usonia community and then moved to Manhattan as their nest emptied. Looking to retirement and grandchildren, they found twenty-four pastoral acres on a lake in Dutchess County, yet remained apprehensive about full-time relocation. GRT Architects proposed to start by building a small studio that would let the clients develop a feel for the land before committing further. In order to locate the studio, a master plan was developed for a three-bedroom house, workshop, swimming pool, firepit, and dock, laying them out to share utilities sized to serve all, including a common drive, septic system, well, and electrical service.

The studio is clad in textured black brick, a material that creates optical illusions depending on lighting, sometimes flattening the complex mass into a single plane. The roof is clad in natural cedar shakes with copper trim intended to add a warmer aspect to the design.

113

A Murphy bed in the living space allows for guests, while tall closets in the sunken sleeping space create some privacy between them and the owners.

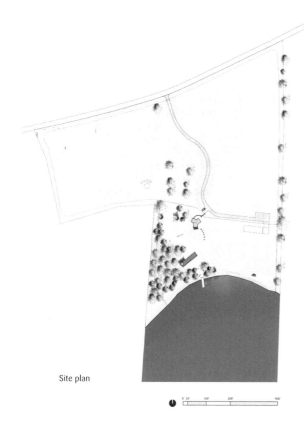

Site plan

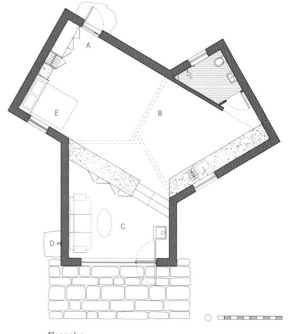

Floor plan

A. Entry
B. Working
C. Living and sleeping
D. Outdoor shower
E. Guest Murphy bed

GRT Architects composed three equally sized volumes in a pinwheel to create an 800-square-foot open plan studio. Each mass has an identical roof atop a beak-like clerestory window, but asymmetry was introduced in response to the site.

The masses meet at a center point, marked by the pinwheel intersection of three steel beams, but the interior is conceived as three subtly implied rooms, each oriented to a different view. The southern mass steps down to follow the topography, and windows are sized and located to balance views with privacy.

114

Built-in cabinets perform many of
the roles walls normally would,
implying rooms without dividing
the space and creating areas for
cooking, living, and sleeping.

The counters are in custom terrazzo, fabricated by KAZA Concrete, who also produces GRT's Flutes & Reeds line of concrete tiles.

The architect bought a 1960s apartment with an excessively partitioned layout and transformed it into the bright, open haven that is now her home. The new design focuses on the fluidity of spaces and, particularly, on the seamless connection between the kitchen, living, and dining areas. In contrast with the exposed raw materials, such as concrete and brick, plants enhance and freshen up the apartment's decor and ambiance. The architect wanted a home where she could simultaneously cook, eat, and be social with her guests. This could only happen in one single space.

Pompeia Apartment

968 sq ft

Pompeia, São Paulo, Brazil

**Nathalia Favaro/
Vitrô Arquitetura**

© Ana Mello

115

The kitchen is open to the living and dining area, reflecting a lifestyle that promotes communication and social interaction.

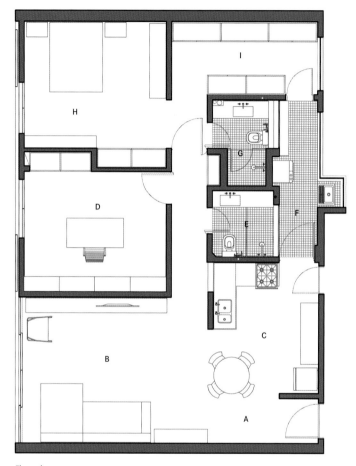

Floor plan

A. Entry foyer
B. Living room
C. Kitchen/dining area
D. Office
E. Bathroom
F. Laundry room
G. Master bathroom
H. Master bedroom
I. Walk-in closet

During demolition, the space started to adopt a very straightforward language of raw materials. Opening up the plan and exposing these materials guided the selection of other finishes and the decor.

116

The clay brick was preserved along the corridor to add visual interest and create focal points. All other walls and ceilings were painted white. The goal was to create a spacious, bright, and comfortable space.

117

A simple color and material palette gives the apartment a sense of flow. Also, with no bulky furniture, not only does the decor reinforce this sense of flow, but it also makes tiny spaces feel roomier.

Stacked Cabin

880 sq ft

Muscoda, Wisconsin,
United States

Johnsen Schmaling Architects

© John J. Macaulay

This small cabin for a young family sits at the end of an old logging road, its compact volume hugging the edge of a small clearing in a remote Wisconsin forest. To minimize the building's footprint and take advantage of the sloped site, the horizontally organized components of a traditional cabin—typically an open-plan longhouse with communal living space, an outhouse, and a freestanding toolshed—were reconfigured and stacked vertically. The bottom level, carved into the hill, houses a small workshop, equipment storage, and a washroom, providing the infrastructural base for the living quarters above. The design takes advantage of readily available materials used in the region's farmstead architecture. On the outside, exposed concrete, cedar, anodized metal, and cementitious plaster all echo the muted, earthy hues of the surrounding forest.

A wood-slatted entry door opens to stairs that lead up to the open living hall centered around a wood-burning stove and bracketed by a simple galley kitchen and a pair of small, open sleeping rooms.

The material palette extends to the inside, where integrally colored polished concrete floors on the two main levels provide sufficiently durable surfaces against the periodic abuse from cross-country skis, dogs, and muddy hiking boots.

A small study, originally conceived as another room adjacent to the living hall, was instead stacked on top of it, creating an intimate, elevated observatory with treetop views.

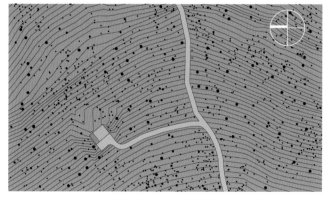

Site plan

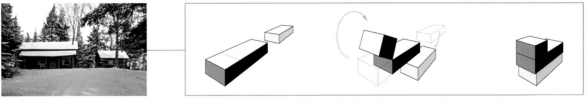

Volumetric morphology diagrams

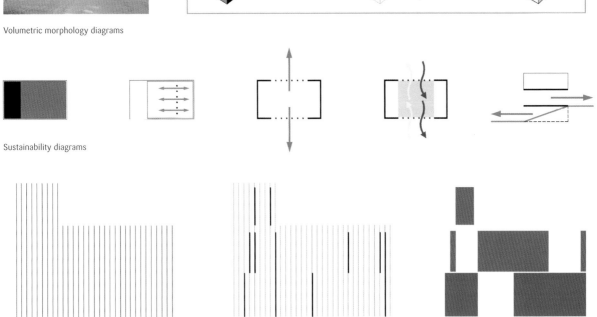

Sustainability diagrams

Facade morphology diagrams

118

In natural settings, reducing the mass of large buildings with small-massing components helps integrate architecture into its immediate surroundings.

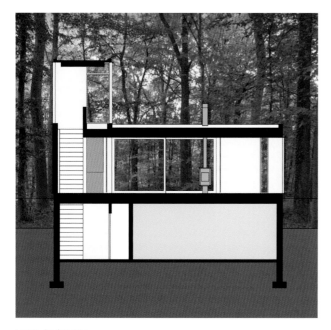

Longitudinal section

Cross section

Exploded axonometric view

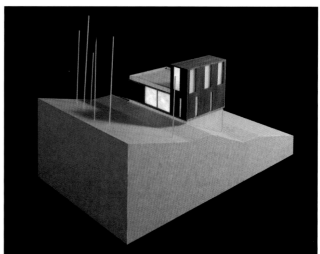

Scale model

376 Stacked Cabin

119

The visual impact is minimized with part of the cabin built into the hillside. This allows for greater usable area relative to a small footprint.

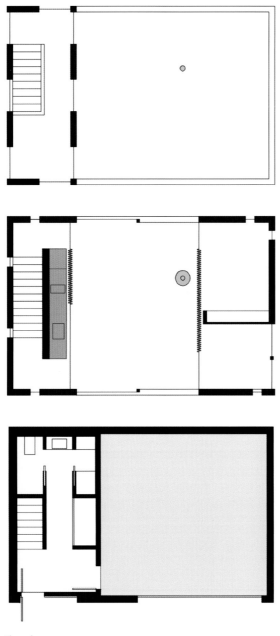

Floor plans

Large-scale lift-slide apertures along the sides of the living hall offer extensive views of the forest and direct access to an informal hillside terrace. In the summer, the apertures become screened openings, virtually transforming the living hall into a covered outdoor room and facilitating a high degree of cross-ventilation that eliminates the need for mechanical conditioning.

120

Floor-to-ceiling curtains on either end of the living hall can be moved or retracted. Depending on their arrangement, the curtains can provide privacy for the sleeping rooms, combine adjacent spaces when opened, or screen the kitchen when not in use; a perfect design solution for tiny spaces where we want to minimize solid and permanent partitions.

Stacked Cabin **379**

Three tiny kiosks stand both poetically and practically on one of Montreal's most beloved landmarks, Mount Royal Park. The uniqueness of the kiosks is the result of their integration into the park in the most discreet and harmonious manner possible. Their design is a delicate balance between the demands of infrastructure and the integration of the buildings into the landscape.

The kiosks were designed to accommodate different functions: one is used for summer and winter class field trips. With enough room for up to 30 people, the possibilities for activities are multifold. A second kiosk houses tools and equipment for park services, as well as a first-aid station. The third is home to the ticket office and is also used as storage for recreational equipment.

Mont-Royal Kiosks

485 sq ft

Montreal, Quebec, Canada

Atelier Urban Face

© Fany Ducharme, Normand Rajotte, Sylvain Legault, and Sylvie Perrault

The light and the constant shifting of the wind inspired the design of the kiosks and led to the expression of a sense of movement. This movement, which follows wind paths and light shifts, is materialized by the kiosks' steel structures.

The transparency also encourages
an interplay of light and shadows,
reinforcing the sense of movement in
the interiors, which, far from feeling
tiny, are experienced as part of the
greater outdoors.

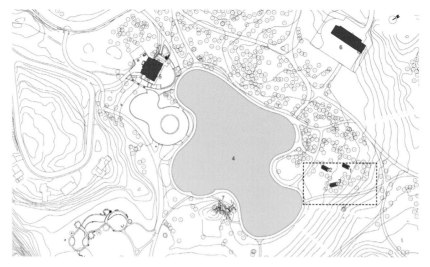

Site plan

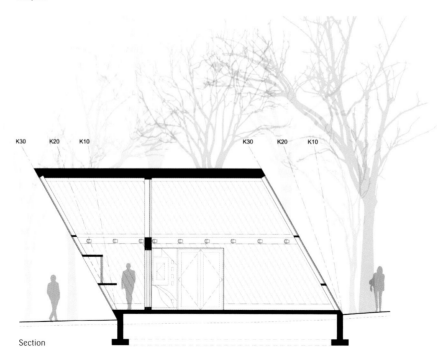

Section

121

The shape, the minimalistic use of materials, and the transparency of the buildings create a sense of lightness and airiness. These qualities ensure optimal integration with their natural surroundings.

The tongue-and-groove board surfaces
stained a neutral color give the interiors
a warm and welcoming feel.

122

The interiors are open, with minimal obstructions, to maximize the spatial experience and make every inch of the small spaces usable.

123

Consolidating storage and utilities
in one central area means that
the space around it can be open,
lending itself to flexible use.

New Affiliates has completed the redesign of a pied-à-terre apartment near New York City's Gramercy Park for a strategic advisor to emerging architects who lives bicoastally. The renovation focused on efficient space planning and flexible programming to provide ample live-and-work space within the confines of a small studio apartment. The apartment will serve as both a part-time residence and space for entertaining and can convert quickly from home to salon, and from private interior to event space.

In plan, the apartment consists of two distinct zones with a bathroom in between, a footprint that imitates that of a larger-size unit in program and feel.

Gramercy Studio

500 sq ft

New York, New York, United States

New Affiliates

© Michael Vahrenwald/Esto

124

Concentrating storage and utilities in one compact and central area can free up valuable floor space.

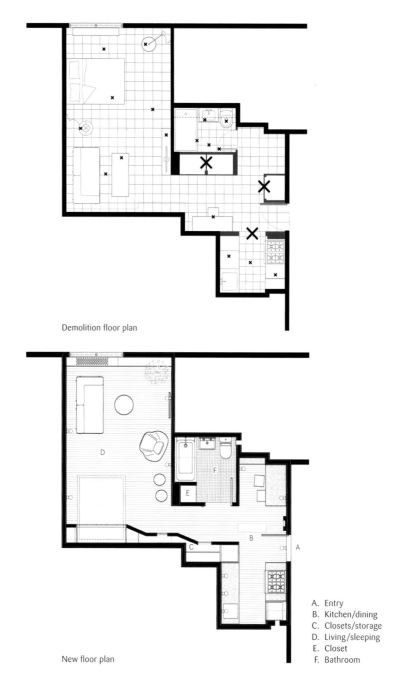

Demolition floor plan

New floor plan

A. Entry
B. Kitchen/dining
C. Closets/storage
D. Living/sleeping
E. Closet
F. Bathroom

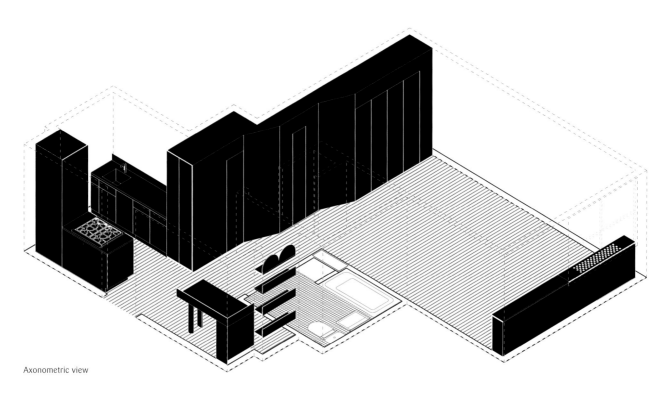

Axonometric view

To optimize space for a range of daily uses, the designers compartmentalized the apartment into a sequence of dual-use areas. A small recess by the entry functions as an office as well as an extension of the adjacent kitchen; the bedroom also serves as a living and/or dining space.

125

Painting furniture the same color
as the walls creates the illusion of
a much bigger space and gives the
furniture a built-in look.

A faceted white wall connects the two main living areas: the hybrid kitchen/office with the back bedroom/living/dining space. This element serves multiple functions. It contains pantry storage, closet space, and a Murphy bed while bouncing natural light from the single window in the apartment throughout the interior.

The color palette made of soft neutral tones, including shades of off-white and pale green, creates an open and airy atmosphere. Custom millwork with faceted and fun forms keeps the project simple while also adding specific moments of character.

126

The bathroom is clad in a small, gridlike 2-inch square tile, and the flooring throughout is white oak in thin, 3-inch planks. These small-scale materials manipulate the apparent proportions of the apartment.

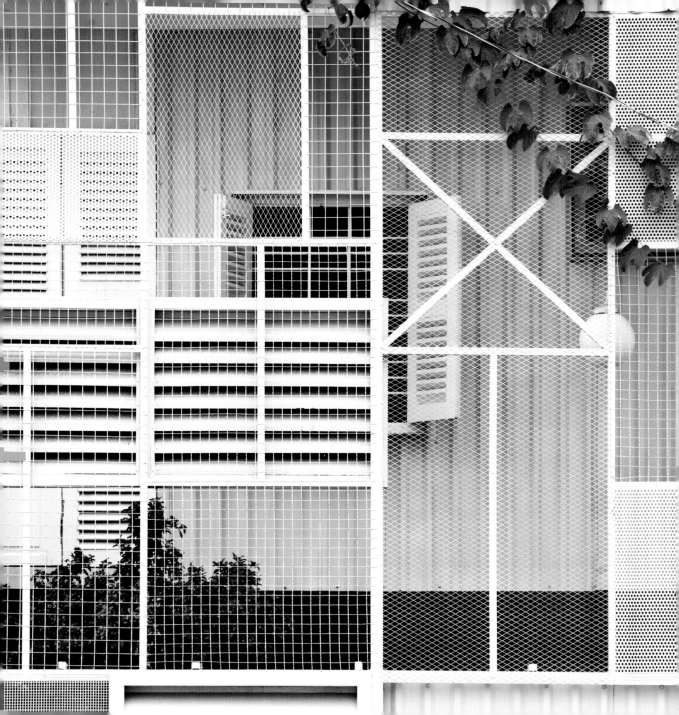

The striking new house design for an architectural journalist in the outskirts of Binh Duong City is a celebration of the area's eclectic architectural context and its compact yet open plan. The design intent was to create a house with a strong connection with nature. Conceptually, the house is conceived as a treehouse or as a nest, hence its name. All the sides of the house have views of the verdant courtyard. This creates a feeling of being perched in a tree canopy and compensates for reduced interior space. Moreover, the ground floor opens up to the exterior, promoting outdoor living. A modest budget guided most design decisions, following principles of sustainability to reduce negative environmental impact.

The Nest

430 sq ft
Binh Duong, Vietnam

a21studio

© Hiroyuki Oki

127

The home is designed for outdoor living, taking advantage of the year-round warm weather and the thriving vegetation. The ground floor is a spacious living area that spills out onto the exterior, only protected by a green canopy.

The house has a double skin. The inner skin is formed by a steel structure clad in corrugated metal panels. The outer skin is conceived as a metal canopy made of different types of grating panels. This canopy serves as a support for creepers and other plants, which eventually will cover the structure, providing the house with shade.

Conceptual diagram. Integration of nature into built environment

Conceptual diagram. Salvaged furniture for environmental sustainability

Conceptual diagram. Living with nature

128

The use of recycled materials and the minimization of energy usage for construction and house maintenance allow for the desire to provide the client with affordable and comfortable living.

129

The design of this budget-conscious house—its flexible spatial organization allowing for future changes and its contact with nature—responds to the growing environmental awareness and the spreading interest in low-cost construction of Vietnamese society.

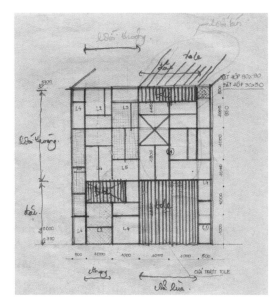

Elevation study

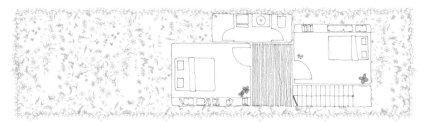

Floor plan

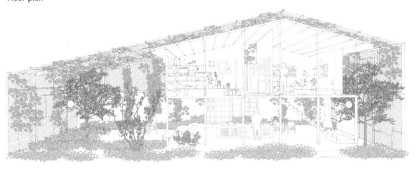

Perspective section

Instead of the more common but more expensive brick and concrete, the architects kept costs down by using premanufactured and recycled materials. The use of these materials and a clever design give the house a distinct character.

The design establishes a contrasting yet harmonious coexistence between the built world and the natural world. The most striking example is the colorful and floral-themed cement tile flooring extending into the courtyard and merging with the lush greenery.

The house is built of recycled furniture
parts and basic construction materials
such as steel, corrugated metal panels,
and expanded metal grating.

In rural West Tisbury, Massachusetts, a graphic novelist needed a place to park and a place to work. The place to park is a black box with a continuous strip of polycarbonate to let light in and expose the framing "branches" that support the upper floor. What sits on top is a cedar-shingled, light-filled studio in the trees. Tall walls with large windows on the east frame views of the surrounding foliage, and low walls with small windows on the west provide privacy from the adjacent main house. The local building restrictions on "detached bedrooms" only allow partitions for a bathroom. Thus, the bathroom, placed in the center of the room, divides the open living layout into two distinct zones of living/working and sleeping, allowing occupants to circulate around both sides.

Tree House

880 sq ft

West Tisbury, Massachusetts, United States

Nick Waldman Studio

© Nick Waldman

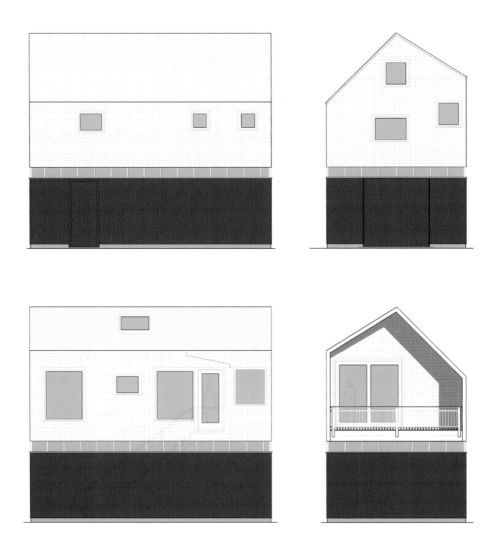

Elevations

The shape of the house and its fenestration responds specifically to the site conditions while maximizing its interior spaces.

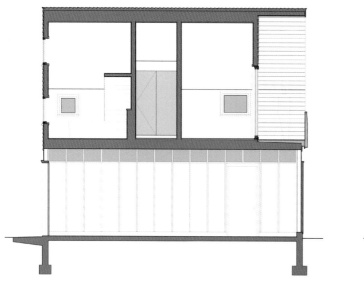

Longitudinal section

Cross section

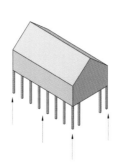

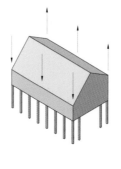

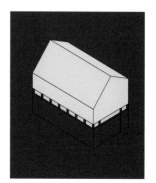

Massing diagrams

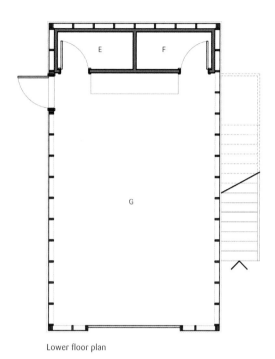

Lower floor plan

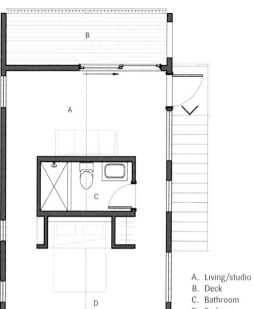

Upper floor plan

A. Living/studio E. Mechanical
B. Deck   room
C. Bathroom   F. Storage
D. Bedroom   G. Garage

131

The living area/studio and the bedroom benefit from daylight and unobstructed views. Because the access staircase to the home is exterior, the entire floor area is usable.

Elevation diagram

Light from a large operable skylight in high ceilings gives the bathroom a very open feel.

A private narrow deck in the back
provides a place to pause and reflect
on the nature that the studio sits in.

aux box

240 sq ft

Parksville, British Columbia,
Canada

aux box

© aux box

Aux box cofounders Morgan Seeber and Landon Sheck
established aux box based on their strong belief that a purposeful,
architecturally beautiful space is paramount to the success of
one's pursuits.

Aux box is an affordable solution that adds customized space to
one's home in the backyard. The aux box can be used as a yoga
studio/gym, writing sanctuary, art studio, guest room, kids' play
area, or home office. Aux box provides access and proximity
to the space individuals and families require—close enough
to eliminate a commute but separated enough to allow for
tranquility and/or focus.

Aux box products require no building permits and are assembled entirely in the company's construction warehouse. Once complete, professional delivery and installation are simple, fast, and clutter-free.

132

Prefabs offer many advantages for people in search of small-scale housing. They are fast to build, affordable, and environmentally friendly thanks to their small footprint, minimal construction waste, and energy efficiency.

For the price of an economy car, people can have the space they need at their doorstep. Better yet, unlike an economy car, the addition of an aux box will increase a home's value.

133

Each aux box includes an infinite number of customizable features, ensuring that the new space reflects everything a person needs to maximize their full potential.

Fenlon House

960 sq ft

Los Angeles, California,
United States

Martin Fenlon Architecture

© Zach Lipp

A dilapidated 1920s bungalow has undergone a major remodel, bringing new life to the old structure. A new addition to the front of the house forms a unique alliance with the refurbished existing home. While the established setbacks limited the porch size, the addition relates nicely with the proportions of the existing house. The porch creates a pleasant sense of entry and a sheltered outdoor space with a bench. Inside, living, dining, and kitchen areas share a single open space, maximizing the spatial experience and providing flexible use. Denuded of its former partitions and dropped ceiling, the home's common spaces feel ample and airy.

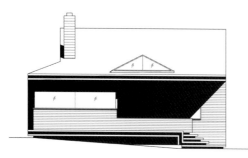

North elevation

West elevation

South elevation

East elevation

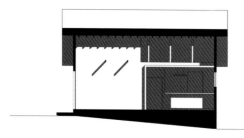

Section AA

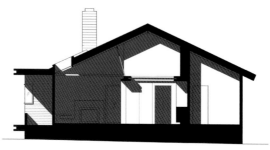

Section BB

The new frontispiece appears to be intimately nested within the older existing house while maintaining a stark differentiation. The frontispiece has been clad in a clear cedar, which contrasts the torched cedar that wraps the rest of the structure. The front addition integrates the house with the adjacent streetscape as it terraces down to the sidewalk and forms a long bench.

134

The original gabled porch roof was removed, leaving a large triangular opening which was turned into a skylight, flooding the interior with natural light and expanding the perception of the small place.

135

Opening up the house interior and stripping it of its dropped ceilings to reveal the wood roof trusses made all the difference. The once overcompartmentalized and dark house was transformed into a space-efficient, bright, and stylish home.

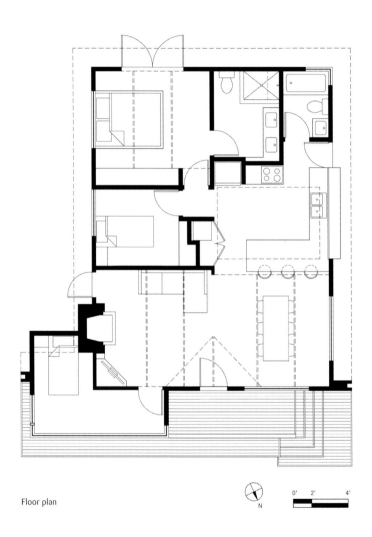

Floor plan

0' 2' 4'

N

136

A large window over the kitchen counter slides open, bringing the outdoors in while allowing the use of the counter from the exterior.

The new walnut and teak finishes throughout are similar in tone to this existing wood, blurring the distinction between old and new. The simple combination of the wood and white plaster throughout is reminiscent of California Mission architecture.

Tall ceilings, light colors, and reflective surfaces—like glass and mirrors—are design features that, combined, create a pleasant, airy, and clean ambiance. In rooms with privacy issues like bathrooms, skylights are a problem solver.

Wee-Ely Cabin

600 sq ft

Superior National Forest,
Minnesota, United States

SALA Architects

© Troy Thies

Designed by SALA Architects and built by Wee Cabin Company,
Wee-Ely stands in an area of rugged cliffs, rocky crags, sky blue
lakes, and marshy bogs near the Boundary Waters Canoe Area
Wilderness, a one-million-acre preserve along the Minnesota
border with Canada. The clients had purchased twenty acres
along the boundary of this preserve and sought an off-grid
shelter surrounded by nature for their family of five. The
architect-builder team satisfied the clients' request, creating
a uniquely handcrafted timber-frame cabin and separate sauna.
Like any other cabins that the Wee Cabin Company builds,
Wee-Ely is customized to meet the clients' needs and budget.

Built similarly to the cabin's construction method, the off-grid, fire-heated sauna provides for personal cleanliness to compensate for the lack of running water in the cabin.

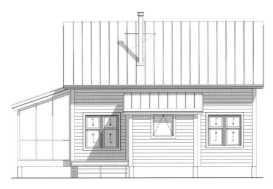

Front elevation

Section

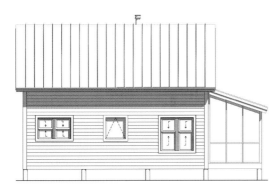

Back elevation

Side elevations

The central structure is three timber-framed bays of 9' × 14'. An 8' × 12' screen porch is on the west end, and a 6' × 9' entry is to the south. Inside, the living space is to the west; kitchen and wood stove in the middle; and dining on the east end. An alternating-tread stair rises to a bridge, with sleeping lofts at each gable end.

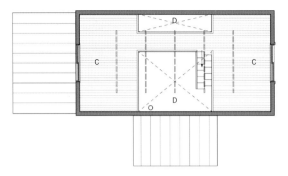

Upper level plan

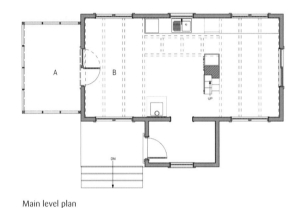

Main level plan

A. Screened porch
B. Loft framing above
C. Loft
D. Open to below

Pier layout

The fir timber-frame structure was cut off-site and assembled on-site. The roof was assembled adjacent to the main frame, complete with windows and metal roofing, and lifted into place with a crane. The frame was infilled and sheathed, exposing the frame inside and out.

The cabin is used in all seasons, with its principal source of heat being the wood stove. Propane gas serves both range and refrigerator. Night light is by candle and gas lantern.

138

Alternating-tread staircases are
excellent space-savers and a
design asset for tiny interiors.

139

Attic spaces are more inviting with windows, skylights, or openings in the floor that allow for visual contact with the floor below, making attics less confined. Sacrificing some floor area does offer advantages, even in tiny spaces.

140

Screened balconies and terraces open interior spaces to the outdoors. Because they are sheltered from the elements, they can be used well beyond the good weather season.

Courtyard DADU is a Detached Accessory Dwelling Unit constructed in the backyard of an early 1900s farmhouse in an urban Seattle neighborhood. The 760-square-foot DADU was designed as a living space for a property owner who plans to rent out the main house.

Oriented around a north-facing courtyard, the DADU's U-shape plan offers privacy from the street and establishes a quiet outdoor space. Creating protection and a sound barrier from the nearby freeway was a central directive driving the design.

Courtyard DADU

760 sq ft

Seattle, Washington, United States

Robert Hutchison Architecture

© Eirik Johnson

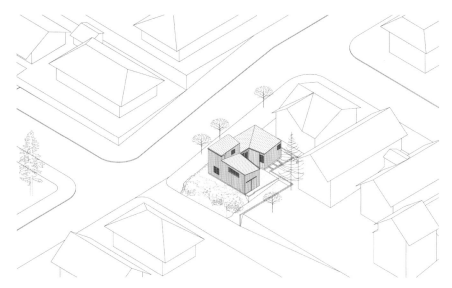

Axonometric view of building site

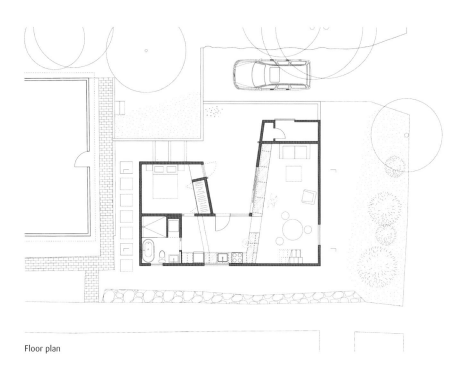

Floor plan

House sections

The U-shape configuration of the house allows for a private outdoor retreat, protected from the winds while adding usable square footage to the small house.

141

A wall-to-wall continuous window bench can include generous storage and provide comfortable seating with cushions. It can also be the right height for a TV screen and display decorative items and books, for instance.

142

Various small spaces oriented toward a central open space give the impression of amplitude. Even more so if these spaces are visually connected, creating long sight lines.

Focusing on key design elements such as the floating platform sleeping loft and the custom stair adds value while maintaining the economy. Bent steel plates form the alternating-tread stairs that seem to hover in space, providing an attractive, space-saving solution for accessing the upper level.

143

When dealing with tiny spaces, small openings, screens, grilles, and low walls are design details that make the difference between tiny, dark, and confined rooms and inviting, bright, and warm spaces.

Set below the street level of a busy street, the Basement Apartment is calm and light-filled, balancing a minimalist approach with the building's heritage. The brief was to create a pied-à-terre with flexibility for executive lease, permanent living, or office use. To achieve the brief, the heritage-listed apartment—which had been badly renovated in the 1980s—was reduced back to its original shell. The new remodel opens the depths of the apartment up to the east light and Sydney city view. This was made possible thanks to the steep slope of the site. The apartment was then reinstated to its original beauty, making the most of the high ceilings.

Basement Apartment

527 sq ft

Potts Point, New South Wales, Australia

Brad Swartz Architects

© Katherine Lu

144

Renovating basement apartments is always a challenge requiring extra thought to meet light and ventilation requirements.

The bathroom—which couldn't be relocated—laundry, essential kitchen appliances, and storage were carefully jigsawed into the back of the apartment. This then allowed the two main rooms of the apartment to be freed up and be used as spacious living areas.

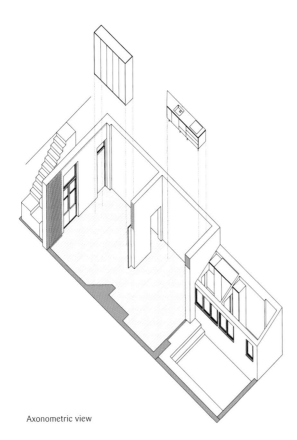

Axonometric view

Floor plan

A. Entry
B. Bedroom
C. Kitchen
D. Dining
E. Living
F. Kitchen/pantry/laundry
G. Bathroom

Small-scale furnishings work well in spaces of reduced dimensions because they are less intrusive and don't block light as much as bigger pieces of furniture.

White is a practical color choice for small areas because it reflects light, increasing the sense of space.

The millwork in the living space and bedroom was kept deliberately slight and elegant, reading more like freestanding furniture so as not to compete with the heritage features and to emphasize the high ceilings.

147

Bathrooms are generally the smallest room in a home. With small windows or none at all to bring in some natural light, small bathrooms can be rather unpleasant. Natural lighting can transform small bathrooms into inviting places where we want to spend time.

Milsons Point Apartment

656 sq ft

Milsons Point, New South Wales, Australia

Brad Swartz Architects

© Katherine Lu

Originally a serviced apartment, this one-bedroom unit was replanned to add a study/guest bedroom without compromising space or taking away from the harbor view. The result is an innovatively transformed apartment designed to accommodate a couple downsizing from a family home. The apartment's millwork creates a functional kitchen, a window seat to take in the views of the Sydney Harbor, and a generous wardrobe in the main bedroom.

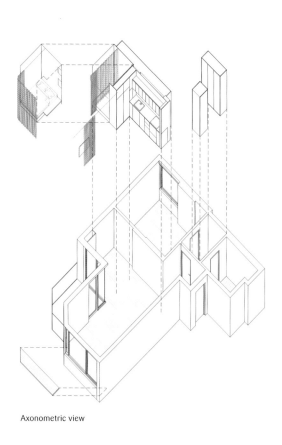

Axonometric view

148

To maximize the functionality of the study/guest room, the design introduced a central joinery unit and snuggly fitted in a double bed that folds away. Also, to create additional storage, the floor was raised.

Existing floor plan

New floor plan

A. Living
B. Dining
C. Kitchen
D. Study/guest bedroom
E. Entry
F. Main bedroom
G. Bathroom

The kitchen was relocated to make space for the study/guest bedroom and to avoid the need for accommodating a desk or retractable bed in the living space.

149

A window bench makes for comfortable sitting to enjoy views and sunlight. Move the dining table over to it, and you have extra seating. Even better, it can have storage underneath.

Long, heavy curtains can be used as space dividers. They can enclose part of a room, turning it into a cozy nook, for example.

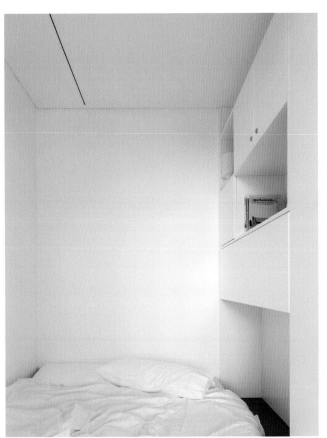

150

Versatility is critical in the design of tiny spaces. It allows for functionality and practicality.

DIRECTORY

Alchemy Architects
Saint Paul, Minnesota, United States
www.alchemyarch.com

Alia Bengana
Paris, France
www.aliabengana.com

Anacapa Architecture
Santa Barbara, California; Portland,
Oregon; United States
www.anacapaarchitecture.com

Architecture Workshop PC
Brooklyn, New York, United States
www.aw-pc.com

a21studio
Ho Chi Minh City, Vietnam
www.a21studio.com.vn

Aurélie Monet Kasisi
Geneva, Switzerland
www.monetkasisi.ch

aux box
Parksville, British Columbia, Canada
www.auxbox.ca

Best Practice
Seattle, Washington, United States
www.bestpracticearchitecture.com

BLAarchitettura
Turin, Italy
www.blaarchitettura.it

Bla Design Group
Vancouver, British Columbia, Canada
www.bla-design.com

B.L.U.E. Architecture Studio
Beijing, China
www.b-l-u-e.net

Brad Swartz Architects
Surry Hills, New South Wales, Australia
www.bradswartz.com.au

COA Mimarlik
Istanbul, Turkey
www.coamimarlik.com

Dean Works Architecture + Design
Brooklyn, New York, United States
www.deanworks.nyc

dontDIY
Sofia, Bulgaria
www.dontdiystudio.com

Fifth Arch
Berkeley, California, United States
www.fiftharch.com

Format Architecture Office
Brooklyn, New York, United States
www.format.nyc

fuseproject
San Francisco, California, United States
www.fuseproject.com

GRT Architects
Brooklyn, New York, United States
www.grtarchitects.com

HANNAH
Ithaca, New York, United States
www.hannah-office.org

ICOSA Design
Oakland, California, United States
www.icosadesign.com

Sinato
Osaka, Japan
www.sinato.jp

Johnsen Schmaling Architects
Milwaukee, Wisconsin, United States
www.johnsenschmaling.com

Martin Fenlon Architecture
Los Angeles, California, United States
www.martinfenlon.com

Michael K Chen Architecture | MKCA
New York, New York, United States
www.mkca.com

Mili Młodzi Ludzie
Poznań, Poland
www.milimlodziludzie.com

mode:lina
Poznań, Poland
www.modelina-architekci.com

Nathalia Favaro/Vitrô Arquitetura
São Paulo, Brazil
www.vitro.arq.br

Nicholas Gurney
Sydney, New South Wales, Australia
www.nicholasgurney.com.au

Nick Roberts, AIA and Cory Buckner, Architect
Los Angeles, California, United States
www.corybuckner.com

Nick Waldman Studio
West Tisbury, Massachusetts, United States
www.nickwaldman.com

Nils Holger Moormann and B&O Group
Aschau im Chiemgau, Germany
www.moormann.de

New Affiliates
New York, New York, United States
www.new-affiliates.us

New Frontier Design
Nashville, Tennessee, United States
www.newfrontiertinyhomes.com

Plant Prefab
Studio: Santa Monica, California,
United States
Headquarters and factory: Rialto, California,
United States
www.plantprefab.com

Perrault Architecture
Montreal, Quebec, Canada
www.perraultarchitecture.ca

Robert Hutchison Architecture
Seattle, Washington, United States
www.robhutcharch.com

Robert Nebolon Architects
Berkeley, California, United States
www.RNarchitect.com

Ruetemple
Moscow, Russia
www.ruetemple.ru

SALA Architects
Minneapolis, Minnesota, United States
www.salaarc.com

Samantha Mink
Los Angeles, California, United States
www.samanthamink.com

3SIXo Architecture
Providence, Rhode Island, United States
www.3sixo.com

Webster Wilson Architect
Portland, Oregon, United States
www.websterwilson.com